Books by Berton Roueché

ELEVEN BLUE MEN

THE INCURABLE WOUND

THE DELECTABLE MOUNTAINS

THE NEUTRAL SPIRIT

A MAN NAMED HOFFMAN

FIELD GUIDE TO DISEASE

WHAT'S LEFT

▼

WHAT'S LEFT

Reports on a Diminishing America

▲

Berton Roueché

WHAT'S LEFT

Reports on a Diminishing America

Boston LITTLE, BROWN AND COMPANY *Toronto*

The contents of this book first appeared
in *The New Yorker*.

Published simultaneously in Canada
by Little, Brown & Company (Canada) Limited

PRINTED IN THE UNITED STATES OF AMERICA

For
William M. Donnelly, Jr.

The opportunity to see geese is more important than television, and the chance to find a pasque-flower is a right as inalienable as free speech.

— ALDO LEOPOLD

Contents

▼▼▼

A Walk on the Towpath

In those vernal seasons of the year, when the air is calm and pleasant, it were an injury and sullenness against nature not to go out, and see her riches, and partake in her rejoicing.

— JOHN MILTON, *in his*
"Tractate on Education," 1644

I WAS DOWN in Washington around the middle of
March, and smelling spring in the air, I gave my-
myself the pleasure of a walk in the country to meet
it. The walk I chose was along the towpath of the
derelict Chesapeake & Ohio Canal. Situated on the
Maryland bank of the Potomac River, the C. & O.
Canal extends from the Georgetown section of
Washington to a natural passage in the Appala-
chians at Cumberland, a distance of a hundred and
eighty-four miles. The C. & O. is an old canal — one
of the oldest lock and mule-drawn-boat canals in the
United States. It is also almost the only one of which
more than a trace survives. It was begun in 1828, it
was completed in 1850, and it remained in operation
until shortly after the First World War. The last
boats moved through its locks in 1924. It was then
stripped of its salvage and abandoned. The depres-
sion saved it from piecemeal sale and certain obliter-

3

ation, and in 1938, through a freak of chance and charity, it was acquired by the federal government. The oldest section of the canal — some twenty wandering miles between the terminus at Georgetown and a point known as Violet's Lock — is now a part of the Washington park system. Its decline has been arrested, and its several locks and lock tenders' houses have all been fully restored. The rest, though reserved as a national monument, has been left to the wild and the weather, and it was there I chose to walk.

I began my walk by car. There is no other ready way to reach the canal once it emerges from the city. A friend with whom I was staying drove me out on his way to work. We passed for a time through an open countryside of rolling pastures and white paddock fences. Then the fences wheeled away and the fields roughened into brush and woods. We came to the head of a rutted lane that wound down the side of a ridge. My friend pulled over and stopped.

"Here you are," he said. "You'll hit the canal just down and around that bend."

I got out. He passed me a lunch that his wife had packed, and a leather-covered flask. I stowed them away in my jacket. "Where am I?" I said.

"Lock 22," he said. "Pennifield's Lock, they call it. Violet's Lock is the next lock up — about three miles from here. Then comes Seneca Creek and Seneca Lock and Aqueduct. That's another mile. After that, it's wilderness all the way to what used to

be Edward's Ferry. You won't want to go any farther than that. Edward's Ferry is a good eight miles
above Seneca. Maybe more. I'll pick you up there
around five." He raised his hand. "Get going," he
said, and drove off.

I watched him out of sight, and then headed
down the lane. It had rained in the night, and the
lane was awash with thin red mud, and puddles stood
in the ruts and potholes. It was steep, wet, slippery
walking. And cold. Under the trees the morning air
had a bite. It felt more like fall than spring. But
from what I could see of the sky overhead, the
clouds were beginning to break and lift, and there
was a hint of a watery sun. I slid down the lane to the
foot of the ridge. A coterie of chickadees burst up
from a thicket and scattered like a handful of gravel.
The lane cut sharply to the left and emerged in a
little meadow. At the edge of the meadow stretched
the canal. Some fifty feet wide, the color of mud, and
flanked by head-high banks, it looked like a sunken
road. The towpath followed the farther bank, and
beyond it, through a heavy screen of trees, I caught a
distant glimpse and murmur of the river. The Canal
lay as still as a pond. I found a pebble and tossed it
in. It sank with a throaty plunk. I guessed the water
to be five or six feet deep. About a hundred yards
downstream, the canal funneled into a kind of open
culvert, which was bridged by a railed catwalk. Facing it, on the towpath side, sat a small white-washed
stone house with two stone chimneys and a pitched

roof of corrugated iron. That would have been the lock tender's house. The culvert was the lock.

I walked out on the bridge and looked down at the lock. The canal flowed into the lock through a sprung wooden gate just under the bridge. It ran between two narrowly confining walls for about a hundred feet. Then, with a sudden boil and bubble, it broke against another gate, spilled through, and resumed its sluggish course. The walls of the lock were faced with big blocks of rust-red sandstone. Some of the stones were so huge they could have been hoisted into place only with a block and tackle. It was beautiful stone, and it had been beautifully finished and fitted. Time had merely softened it. Here and there along the courses I could even make out the remains of a mason's mark. One device was quite distinct — a double-headed arrow. Another appeared to be two overlapping equilateral triangles. I went on across the bridge to the house. The windows were shuttered and boarded up, and the door was locked. No matter. It was enough just to stand and look at it. It was a lovely house, as beautifully made as the lock, and as firmly designed for function. It gave me a pang to think that there had once been a time when even a lock tender could have so handsome a house. A phoebe called from a sweet-gum tree in the dooryard. Far away, somewhere down by the river, a mourning dove gave an answering sigh. I looked at my watch. It was ten minutes after ten. I started up the towpath.

The sun was still no more than a promise, but the air had lost its chill. It was going to be a spring day after all. The signs of it abounded. Most of the trees that lined the path — sycamore, dogwood, sweet gum, hickory, elm — were coming into bud. Only the oaks still had the wrought-iron look of winter. Some creeping vine — Virginia creeper or honeysuckle — was even in leaf. And everywhere there were birds in sight or sound. Robins hopped and stood and listened at intervals along the way. A woodpecker drummed. A blue jay raced from tree to tree, screaming a wild alarm. There was a flash of cardinal red across the canal. I turned — but too late. It was gone. And so were the lock and the house. They had vanished around a bend. There was nothing behind me but water and woods. It gave me a curious sensation. I felt for the first time completely alone, but I didn't feel lonely. It was an exhilarating loneliness. It was solitude. I took a deep breath and lighted a cigarette. I felt at peace with the world.

But peace was mine alone. Every step I took spread panic. The sentinel jay was joined by a dozen agitated crows. A terrified rabbit sprang out from behind a fallen tree and ran for its life up the path. I had no choice but to follow it. It erupted again almost under my feet. This time, more sensibly, it took to the woods. I watched it bounding through the brush, changing its course with every bound, and finished my cigarette. I pitched the butt into the canal. There was a tiny splash near the water's edge. I stepped to the bank and looked down and around. Nothing moved but the drifting cigarette. A long minute passed. Then, a foot or two off the opposite shore, the water just perceptibly stirred. The top of a little black head appeared, and then two bright eyes — a muskrat. We exchanged an inscrutable glance. I moved up a step for a better look. The muskrat disappeared without a ripple.

I resumed my walk. Across the canal, the ridge stiffened into a rocky cliff. Pines and cedars grew among the rocks, and the rocks were green with lichen. The canal edged away from the cliff and the river woods thinned out, and the river swept majestically into view. It was high and wide and moving fast. Across the river, beyond a scrubby island, a cloud of gulls hung over the Virginia bluffs. In the slack water at the foot of the island sat a pair of swans. A tremulous whistle recalled me to Maryland. It came from somewhere across the canal, from somewhere up on the cliff, and it sounded something like a redwing. It wasn't a redwing, though. It was a call I had never heard before. I listened, and it came again. It had almost the sound of a blue note. I waited. But the second call was the last. I gave up, and went on. Another phoebe called, and another blue jay screamed another warning. Another woodpecker drummed. The sun began to brighten. And then I heard the river. It was no longer merely a murmur. It was rising into a rumble. The rumble became a roar. That could only mean rapids ahead. A moment later, I saw them — a tumult of dirty white water thrashing down through a rubbly race between the bank and a cluster of islands. But I hardly got more than a glimpse. The path and the river were now a scant twenty feet apart, and the view was abruptly blocked by a levee of earth and rock and hedgerow scrub that rose as high as my head. I walked along the lee of the levee in the enveloping roar of the rapids for almost half a mile. Then, slowly, the roar subsided. It rumbled and grumbled and faded away to a murmur as still as silence. The levee petered out in a tumble of brush, and the river serenely returned. Trees reappeared on its broadening bank and mounted to the edge of the path. I heard a dribble of running water. The towpath took a turn. Just around the turn were a clearing, a footbridge, and a lock — Violet's Lock.

Violet's Lock was a ruin. The sound I had heard was river water flowing into the canal through a silted inlet some yards below the lock. The bridge I had seen was a towpath bridge across the inlet. There was nothing left of Violet's Lock but two walls spanned by a plank. The lock gates were gone, and the lock tender's house had vanished without a trace. I turned away, and saw two fishermen squatting on the riverbank. Both were Negroes and both were wearing shiny windbreaker jackets with Chinese dragons embroidered on the back. One jacket was purple, the other green. The man in the purple jacket gave me a friendly salute.

"What's biting?" I said.

"Man," he said, "don't ask *me* that. I'm just standing here with this line in my hand."

"Cat," the other man said. "I got me one just a little while back." He reached under a bush and held up an eight-inch catfish strung on a willow twig. "It don't amount to much."

"I'm just standing here," the first man said. "I'm just holding this line in my hand."

"Cat's about all you can count on now," the other man said. "Or suckers. But there's carp out there. Big carp. And bass — " He let out a sudden grunt. His line tautened and twitched. He rose to a crouch and gave his rod a jerk. He reeled in a catfish twice the size of the other. "Well, looky there," he said.

"I'm looking, man," the first man said. "That's all I've got to do is just stand here and look."

The other man unhooked the fish, thrust a twig through its gills, and tossed it under the bush. "Cat are funny," he said. "I got that first one on chicken liver. That's what they really like. Some people say that's *all* they like. But this one took a worm. Now I wonder should I try a worm again."

"I'll tell you what I wonder," the first man said. "I wonder how long I'm going to stand here with this line in my hand. I wonder when my turn is going to come."

"No," the other man said. "It's liver they really like. I reckon I'll go back to liver."

I wished them both luck, and moved on.

Above Violet's Lock, the canal was a different canal. It had shrunk to a chain of ponds and puddles, and brush and even sapling trees were growing in its bed. Everything was different. The river broadened until the farther shore was only a haze of horizon. Across the canal, the rocky heights turned into hills and drew half a mile or more away. A stretch of boggy woods appeared, and then patches of marsh alive with caroling peepers. Dandelions bloomed along the path. I passed a clump of what looked like chives. A little farther on was another. Then, suddenly, the clumps were everywhere, swarming up and over the path like day lilies escaped from an abandoned garden. I tore up a clump and sniffed the satin leaves and felt the bulbous root. The leaves had an oniony smell, but the bulb was a cluster of segments. I broke it open, and realized what I had found. The path between Violet's Lock and Seneca Creek was a herbalist's paradise of wild garlic. I pulled up a dozen clumps and put the bulbs in my pocket as a present for my friend and his wife.

It was nearly noon when I reached Seneca Creek. I had thought of Seneca as a possible place to sit down and eat my lunch. One look was enough to change my mind. There was another handsome lock tender's house there. There was a lock and an aqueduct that carried the canal across the creek on three handsome stone arches. There was also a splendid view of the river. That, however, was only part of Seneca. The creek was lined with summer cottages and upended rowboats and real-estate signs and old beer cans and bottles. Off to one side were a big parking lot and a gimcrack summer hotel. The resort was deserted now, but it was easy to imagine it in another month or two. I walked past the lock and paused at the aqueduct. Except for the underpinning of arches, it looked much like a lock — a dry and gateless lock. An arrow mason's mark of the sort I had seen at Pennifield's was visible on one of its inner walls, and there were several deep grooves on the sandstone lip of the wall adjoining the path. They had, I supposed, been worn there over the years by the rub of countless towropes.

The peeper marshes and the river woods closed in again. I was back in the cloistered peace of the morning. Beyond the marshes and a screen of trees I caught a glimpse of a low red sandstone bluff. That was probably the source of the stone that built the locks. A downy woodpecker dipped across the canal and into the woods. The woodpecker drumming I had been hearing was probably a downy woodpecker. I all but stepped on a little wood turtle. It crouched under its heraldic carapace with antediluvian patience. I bent down to examine its markings, and there, an inch from its vanished nose, lay a tarnished dime. I pocketed the dime. I picked up the turtle and carried it, with thanks, to its destination on the other, side of the path, and continued on my way. The sun burned through the last of the clouds. A glaze of dusty blue spread over the sky, and the muddy canal faded from brown to a mustard yellow. It was almost hot. I began to look for a place to take my nooning.

It required nearly a mile of looking. The edge of the canal was too prickly with brush, and from what I could see of the woods their floor was a jungle of vine-choked seedlings. I finally found what I wanted in a clearing hacked out by a toppled sycamore. It led to the riverbank and an enormous mossy boulder. Near the boulder was a greening willow tree with a cascade of branches trailing out into the water. I sat down in the dappled shade of the willow and leaned back against the boulder. I was tired. For a moment, I simply sat there. I hadn't known how tired I was. But I was also limp with hunger. I got out the lunch that my friend's wife had prepared, and opened the pocket flask. I sniffed and felt better and took a swallow. It was wine — *rosé*. I unpacked my lunch. She had given me a roast-beef sandwich, a Swiss-cheese sandwich, a fried chicken leg, and a hard-boiled egg. The egg was still in its shell, and on the shell she had drawn a grinning pumpkin face. It seemed a shame to immediately shatter so nice a surprise. I put the egg aside and ate the sandwiches and the chicken leg, and washed them down with the wine. But I was still hungry. I cracked the egg and ate it with a pinch of salt and pepper that I found in a twist of foil. I lighted a cigarette and finished off the wine, and watched the river roll by.

My eye was caught by a duck in the water. It sat drifting along on the current just offshore, and I recognized it as a diving duck — a tiny bufflehead. The bufflehead is one of the smallest and loveliest of ducks, but it wasn't its beauty that caught and held my eye. It was its posture. Its body was headed upstream; it was coming down tailfirst. I watched it with astonishment, and then with a kind of alarm. It was floating straight for the trap of trailing willow branches. Another few feet, a few more seconds, and it would be in among them. I waited for it to dive or change its course. But it seemed entirely oblivious. It sailed brainlessly into the trap. A branch touched its back. It swung around, gave a petulant squeak, and dived. A moment passed. I scanned the water above, beyond, and below the willow. There was a squeak from under the tree. The duck was back exactly where it had been before. It submerged again. This time, it came up in open water, but its situation was not much improved. It was upstream of the tree once more, and only just clear of the branches. The touch of a branch sent it into another dive. It was down for what seemed like a minute. And this time it surfaced in safety — well beyond the willow and several feet below it. It turned slowly around a time or two. Then, fixing its gaze on some distant point upriver, it let the current take it. It sailed away, and out of sight, tailfirst.

I stood up and stretched. It was time to go. My watch said twenty minutes to two, and I still had a walk of six or seven miles ahead of me. I dug a hole and buried my litter and walked back through the clearing to the towpath. The peepers were still peeping in the marsh. A big fox sparrow ducked out of sight in a thicket. The character of the woods began to change. They had an older, darker, more primitive look, and most of the trees were festooned with monstrous grapevines. They looped and drooped and hung over the path like inextricably tangled ropes. Many of the vines were as thick as my wrist. Some were the size of my ankle. I caught hold of one that dangled from a branch near the edge of the canal and was tempted beyond my age. I gave it a tug. It would easily bear my weight. I got a good grip and moved back a few steps. There was nobody looking. I took a run and a jump, and swung into the air — over the path, over the bank, out over a patch of canal. And back. I let go, stumbled, and landed hard on my rump. I climbed to my feet. I seemed to be all right. No broken bones. No bruises. No harm done. I brushed myself off and moved briskly on up the path. I wasn't even out of breath. I was only out of countenance.

A tremulous whistle sounded overhead. It was the blue-note bird again. I stopped dead in my tracks and peered cautiously up through the trees. Another whistle. Something moved, or seemed to move, high up in a twisted hickory, but I was looking into the sun, and it could have been anything — a branch, a vine, a shifting shadow. I waited in a vacuum of silence. Another movement, another call, and I might be able to place it. The silence broke in a thump of approaching hoofs. Well, that took care of that. I shrugged, and moved on. Two girls on horseback came trotting into view down the path. They were riding abreast, but at the sight of me they reined up, and one dropped back. The lead rider was an easy, smiling, golden girl in jodhpurs and a lavender turtleneck sweater. She smiled and waved. I backed off the path.

"Hi there," she said, and stepped her horse neatly past me.

Her companion wore blue jeans and sneakers. She was dark and grim and hanging on for dear life. She gave me a hurried glance.

"Don't kick now," she said to her horse. "Please don't kick."

I shrank farther into the brush that lined the bank. The golden girl waited for her companion to lurch abreast, then touched her horse back to a trot. They jogged out of sight toward Seneca, and I continued on my way. The marks of their passage were all over the path. At one point, the track was scarred in a wild and ragged circle, and there were several hoofprints precariously close to the brink of the canal. It could have been an awkward drop. The canal was no longer a trickle of ponds and puddles. It was wider and deeper and looked almost like a canal again. Before long, I thought I saw why. The marsh rose into a scrubby field, and at the foot of the field it drained into a little brook. But I was mistaken. I should have known that the canal had been better engineered than that. The brook didn't flow into the canal. It flowed under it and on to the river through a culvert. There must be another inlet at Edward's Ferry or beyond. I heard a crash of wings and a bedlam of squeaks and squawks, and a dozen wood duck exploded from the water. They beat up the canal, just skimming the surface, and wheeled sharply into the woods. Across the canal, the scrub thickened and then was choked abruptly off at a barbed-wire fence. Beyond the fence was a pasture that stretched ahead as far as I could see. A green-and-white striped horse van stood tilted under a big elm near the canal, and in the distance, on the slope of the ridge, stood a broad white house with a façade of six white columns. It looked as if I had emerged from the wild.

I had. After about a mile, the pasture rolled away behind a sycamore grove, and the canal swung back toward the river. Through the trees up ahead I could see the rusty roof and double chimneys of a lock tender's house. Then the river woods opened into a clearing, and a shantytown of shacks and sheds and broken-down trailers mounted on cement blocks appeared. One of the trailers had a wooden sign nailed over the door: CAMP FUN. A man in a blue yachting cap and a sweatshirt was sitting on the doorstep. He stood up when he saw me, and stared. He shambled across the yard, still staring. At the same moment, a little brown dog with a terrier face and the tail of a collie came yapping around the trailer. The man turned.

"Shut up," he said, and gave the dog a kick in the ribs.

The dog sat down. It opened its mouth and yawned. The man came up to the edge of the path.

"Nice day," he said.

"Yes," I said. "Very nice."

"You live around here?" he said.

"No," I said. "I'm just taking a walk along the canal."

"Is that right?" He leaned against a tree. "I live up at Poolesville. But I got me this camp down here at the Ferry."

I looked at my watch. It was almost five o'clock. "Well," I said, and turned to go.

A blue-note whistle came from across the canal. I turned back.

"Did you hear that?" I said. "That whistle?"

"Sure," he said. "What about it?"

"What is it?" I said.

"That?" he said. He looked at me, and shrugged. "Some bird, I reckon."

▼▼▼

A Day on the River

▲▲▲

Montauk Springs, in Dent County, Missouri, and flows south some hundred and eighty miles to a point near Pocahontas, in northern Arkansas, where it joins the Black River, a sub-tributary of the Mississippi. It is a wild highland river, fed entirely by springs and spring-fed creeks, and the country it cuts through, though settled as early as 1800, is still largely unspoiled. In 1962, in order to keep it unspoiled, the Department of the Interior proposed to incorporate about a hundred miles of the river (and all of its tributary Jacks Fork) into a preserve to be called the Ozark National Rivers.* That was why I had come down to Missouri. I had heard about the Current a few months before from friends in Washington, and they had made me want to see it. Its waters are cold, clean, clear, and fast. For much of its length, it has a fall of eight or nine feet a mile. Its upper reaches are the steepest, and also the wildest and the least accessible. Dugan's Landing is one of the few good landings on the upper river and is the only landing within easy reach of Eminence (pop. 516), the seat of Shannon County and the chief town in the area. Beck, a young storekeeper who doubles as a guide and boatman, lives in Eminence, and it was there, by prearrangement, that he and Hall and I had met at about eight o'clock. Hall is around sixty, a naturalist and writer, and the proprietor of Possum Trot Farm, near Caledonia, a couple of counties to the northeast. He was wearing two red flannel

* It became part of the National Park System in 1964.

22

hunting shirts, leather-faced pants, and Wellington boots. Beck had on a khaki jacket and tan, pointed city shoes. Our plan was to spend the day on the river and then put in for supper and the night at a hunting cabin a number of miles downstream owned by a friend of Hall's named Wendell Howard. It was now a little after nine.

Beck's share of the gear was an outboard motor. He shouldered it down the bank to one of the johnboats and clamped it into place on the stern frame. I followed him aboard with the fuel tank and a canoe paddle. In the shade of the clearing, the air had a wintry edge, but here, on the beach in the sun, it was almost balmy. It was going to be a lovely day. I enjoyed its promise for a moment, and then went back and helped Hall with the rest of the gear — a duffel bag, a leather carryall, a fly rod in a canvas case, a Thermos jug of water, and lidded picnic basket. Beck started the motor and brought it to a sputtering roar. He throttled it down to a warming idle, raced it again, and abruptly shut it off. There was an instant of bottomless silence. It was broken by a blue-jay cry from a willow thicket at the foot of the bluff. The morning air stirred through the sycamores, and the sound of the rapids returned. Beck tilted the outboard back on its hinges until the propeller cleared the water. He took up the paddle and nodded to Hall and me to shove off. We shoved. It was a big boat, at least twenty feet long, and four feet wide at the beam, but johnboats are built for easy handling, and one good shove was enough. It slid off the beach and into the water as lightly as a canoe. Hall hopped into the bow. I scrambled after and over and past him, and sat down on the center thwart. Beck leaned on his paddle, and we swung out into the river and into a gentle current. It swept us gently off.

But not for long. We drifted around a wooded point, and a stony bluff rose up on the right. The river began to shoal, and I could feel the current quicken. The sound of the rapids grew louder. I looked around at Beck. He had risen to his feet and was balanced on the stern frame like a gondolier, his paddle poised for a guiding thrust. There was a spume of white water up ahead. Then, with a thump, we were in it. The boat shot forward like a sled on ice. We slicked over a sunken log. We skinned past a seething snag. We slapped and shuddered down a corrugation of bowling-ball boulders. And emerged in a long, placid, sun-swept pool. The bluff on the left had vanished. In its place were a gravel beach and a wall of marshy woods.

Beck shipped his paddle. He sat down and lit a cigarette. "Well, that was Number One," he said. "Dugan's Chute, they call it. It isn't the trickiest chute we'll hit today. Or the roughest or the longest. But it isn't the easiest, either."

"I wouldn't want to run it at night," Hall said. He slipped the fly rod from its case and began to fit it together. "Not on a dark night, anyway."

"That's for a fact," Beck said. "Chutes are

funny. I know some I could run about any old time. If you know them, you know them. I mean, they never change. Others are just the opposite. Those cotton pickers are different every season. Every month, almost."

"How many will we hit today?" I asked.

"Chutes?" he said. "Well, now. It's about twenty-five miles from here to Wendell Howard's place. So I'd say fifteen or twenty chutes. They average close to one a mile — " He broke off, and reached for the paddle. "You see that, Len? Over under the bluff? A bass hit something."

"I saw it," Hall said. He had the rod assembled now and was tying on a spinner and a hairy black fly. "Let's get over there."

We moved silently out of the current and glided toward the bluff. There was a deep hole there. The bottom shelved from three to six to twelve or fifteen feet, but the water was so clear that I could still see every mossy stone and plastered leaf. A big yellow sucker darted under the shadow of the boat. Below it, a waterlogged twig gave a mysterious twitch and turned mysteriously over.

"O.K.," Hall said. "That's fine." He stood up and cast, and waited. He retrieved his line, and cast again. I saw the line go taut. It held steady for an instant, and then knifed away upstream. Hall halted the run with a whip of the rod and the line cut off on another tack. He stopped it short and began to bring in the line, the tip of his rod bending almost double.

There was a splash some thirty feet away. A long moment passed. Another eruption exploded just off the bow of the boat. Hall let out a triumphant grunt, and lifted an arching, twisting, shimmering foot-long smallmouthed black bass. The thwart I was sitting on formed the lid of a built-in live-box, and I slid off and opened it up. Hall unhooked the bass and dropped it into the box.

"Not bad," Beck said. "Just over a pound, I'd say. I like that size."

"I thought he'd be twice that big," I said. "He gave you quite a fight."

"Well," Hall said, "you know what they say about bass — 'Inch for inch and pound for pound, the gamest fish that swims.'"

"That's always been a real good hole," Beck said. "There could be more in there."

It was still a good hole. In a dozen casts, Hall landed two more bass. One was about the size of the first. The other was a trifle larger. Smallmouthed bass can weigh as much as four or five pounds, but these were just right for us. Three pounds or so of bass would make a very fine lunch.

Beck brought the boat about. I could feel the fish sloshing around in the live-box under my seat. We moved out of the hole and the shade of the bluff, and back into the sunny flow of the river. A gaudy male shoveler sat feeding in the shallows off the gravel beach. Its wet green head came up at our approach, and it fixed us with a bold, indifferent eye until we were hardly twenty feet away. Then it was up and off and gone around a bend. We drifted after it on a just perceptible current. The trees that crowned the bluff were shifting and shaking in a gusty breeze, but only a breath of it reached the river, and the air was almost balmy. Hall had already stripped off one of his flannel shirts. I unbuttoned my jacket and took off my cap and enjoyed the feel of the sun on my face. The pool ended in a pinch of beach and bluff, a surge of current, another chute. Beck half rose to his feet, and then sank back again. It was a short, quick, unchallenging chute, and we were down in a single lurch. But just beyond it boiled another. Momentum carried us across an intervening pool. This time, Beck stood up. There was another surge, a yawing slide, a burst of spray, and a thump. The river resumed its broad, unhurried course.

Hall turned his head and caught my eye. He cocked a thumb toward the bluff. I looked where he was pointing — at the chalky hulk of a dead sycamore. Near the top of the tree hung an enormous black-and-white bird with a commanding bright-red crest. It was a bird of a kind I had never seen before, but I knew it at once. It could only be a pileated woodpecker.

"That's right," Hall said. "And a sight to see, isn't he? Simply beautiful. It's also one that not many people ever get these days. Except in country like this. If the ivory-billed woodpecker is extinct — and I guess it pretty well is — the pileated woodpecker is the only big woodpecker left. I'm sure it is. Thank God we've still got this one. Just look at the size of him. He's as big as a crow."

"And as cagey," Beck said. "He's not going to let us get much closer. He'll — See what I mean? There he goes!"

"We'll come across another," Hall said. "I've seen as many as twenty of them along this river in a single day. They're not as demanding as the ivory-bills were. The experts estimate that a pair of ivory-bills needed around six square miles of the wildest kind of forest land to range in. Not because they were so big. Actually, they were only a trifle bigger than the bird you just saw. Their diet — a certain kind of bark beetle — was that special. A pair of pileated woodpeckers can live on a couple of acres or less. It's a wilderness woodpecker, though. You won't find it in the suburbs with the downies and the hairies and the flickers. It needs wild country."

"We've still got plenty of that," Beck said. "I know a couple of stretches here that are as wild as country can get. Bee Bluff is one — the country back of it, especially. You'll see Bee Bluff directly. It isn't but a few miles farther on. The other is what they call Cardareva Mountain. Cardareva is just below Wendell Howard's place, and it's really wild. I've seen an eagle working there. A bald eagle, I guess it was."

"Probably," Hall said.

"There's also bear on Cardareva," Beck said. "A few, anyway. Or so I hear. And wolves. I know we've got some bobcat. I've seen them myself here and there. As a matter of fact, there's still a bounty on wolves and bobcat. The state pays fifteen dollars for a wolf, and a bobcat is worth five. And, of course, there's deer all over the place."

"This country is full of wildlife," Hall said. "There's a gravel bar along here somewhere that my wife and I camped on one time a few years back. I don't think we got a wink of sleep. We shared it with sixteen owls — barred owls. They hollered at us all night long."

"There isn't much we haven't got," Beck said. "Even badger. They tell me those cotton pickers are rarer than bear. I've never seen one myself, but they're still around. Then there's fox and skunk and possum and coon — lots of coon. Coon are thicker than rabbits lately. I don't know what's happened. It used to be you were lucky to get two or three coon in a season. Now, if you've got a good dog, you can get yourself that many in a night. Another thing that's come back strong is turkey — wild turkey. Big ones, too. Gobblers up to thirty pounds."

"Wendell Howard has a good wild-turkey story," Hall said. "He says he was out with a shotgun one afternoon a couple of years ago. He caught sight of a big old gobbler sitting in a clearing, and got up his gun and fired. Only it wasn't a turkey. It turned out to be a stump. But it still looked so much like a turkey, Wendell says, that he gave it the other barrel."

"That sounds like Wendell," Beck said. "Another thing you see along here is mink. And flying squirrels. And muskrat — plenty of muskrat."

"And beaver," I said.

"Beaver?" Beck said.

I pointed to a clump of cottonwoods at the mouth of a slough up ahead. On one of the trees was a deep, fresh, wedge-shaped cut. It was clean enough to have been made with an axe.

Beck grinned. "And beaver," he said.

The river edged around a bend and under a cavernous overhang of bluff. There was a gust of cavelike cold. The arching limestone walls were stained with lichen, and the water was a frosty deep blue-green. It was suddenly winter again. I lit a cigarette. Then the river took another turn, and the stony ceiling lifted and the sun came comfortingly back. A sprawling towhead island, thick with cottonwoods and willow scrub, emerged beyond the turn. It spread almost from bank to bank, and from the passage on the right came the sound of white water.

"That sounds like a rough one," I said.

Hall nodded. "If it's the one I think it is, it's plenty rough."

"Bland Chute, they call it," Beck said. "And it is rough — the roughest. More boats turn over here than any chute on the river. But you have to take it.

The one on the left there is worse. It's blocked. It's a dead end." He rose to a kind of crouch. "Watch yourselves, now." He swung his paddle. "We go right in under the bluff. Watch those branches."

The boat gave a leap into space. It landed with a bone-jarring thump in a boiling trough between two rocks, and slid into space again. We heeled into a long, steep, winding race. I ducked an overhanging branch. A curtain of water rose and fell, and my cigarette disintegrated in my hand. We plunged away from the bluff and over a grinding shoal. The chute began to widen. It began to slow. The island shrank and vanished, and we were back again on the easy, open river. There was an inch of water slopping around my feet. Hall tossed me a bailing sponge, and I soaked and squeezed and sopped the boat dry.

Beck touched me on the shoulder. "I mentioned Bee Bluff a while back," he said. "Well, that's it — that big bluff down there at the bend."

He was pointing at a looming precipice that climbed to a height of at least three hundred feet and stretched away along the river as far as I could see. Its face was scarred with crumbling ledges and brushy caves and crevices sprouting tortured trees, and even in the full gaze of the sun it had a wild, forbidding look. The foot of the bluff was rank with lizardtail weed, and clinging to many of the clinging trees were scraggly beards of some pale-green, hairlike lichen that much resembled Spanish moss. Some of the trees were den-trees, with woodpecker holes

and squirrel holes and holes big enough to accommo-
date a coon or a possum. An osprey drifted out over
the river. I watched it hovering on a lift of heated
air and caught a glimpse of something white on a
ledge near the top of the bluff. It moved, hopping
nimbly across a break in the ledge, and took shape —
a goat. It was followed at a little distance by another. They picked their way along the ledge toward
a screen of cedars, and behind them came a third.
Then a fourth appeared. And a fifth and a sixth. It
became a procession of goats. I counted fourteen in
all. They stepped along the face of the bluff with the
grace and sureness of Rocky Mountain bighorns. It
was a lovely, stirring, dizzying sight.

"They're not as wild as they look," Beck said.
"Only about half. They belong to somebody back in
some hollow somewhere. He lets them browse where
they can. This country is all open range."

It was almost one o'clock, and time for lunch.
Beck began to look for a gravel bar that would make
a comfortable camp. He found one a couple of miles
and three chutes below Bee Bluff. It was open and
sunny but screened from the wind by a grove of
trees, and there was an abundance of driftwood and
brush for fuel just above the high-water mark. We
beached the bow of the boat and unloaded the gear
we would need. A few steps up from the water lay a
ten-foot log as thick as my thigh. We found another
log almost as thick, and dragged it close and parallel

to the first to form the frame of a cooking fire. Hall spread a tarpaulin ground cloth on the pebbly gravel and began to unpack the picnic basket. Beck returned to the boat to clean the fish. I watched him for a minute. He reached into the live-box, brought out a bass, and knocked it on the head. He laid his paddle across the gunwales and stretched the fish out on the blade, and scaled and gutted it with a sheath knife. He tossed the offal overboard. The blade of the paddle made an excellent cleaning block. When the first fish was gutted, he dipped the paddle in the water and washed it clean for the next. I left him then and headed up the beach. My job was to gather firewood. It felt good to be up and moving around after so many hours of sitting. I filled my arms with wood and walked on to the edge of the grove and looked in among the trees. The trees were mostly scarlet oak and shagbark hickory, many of them still hung with leathery last-year's leaves, and I could hear squirrels scratching for nuts in the litter. A nuthatch ran headfirst down a drooping hickory branch. It stopped and stared, and cawed like a tiny crow.

I walked back to the camp. A fire of twigs and splinters was burning between the two big logs, and near it stood an enamelware pan, a blackened coffeepot, and a skillet containing a lump of slowly liquefying bacon fat. Hall was squatting on the edge of the tarpaulin, opening a bottle of Jim Beam. Spread out before him was an array of food — a loaf of bread, a jar of butter, a jar of sugar, an unopened can of vegetable soup and another of peaches, a wedge of rat-trap cheese, and the bass laid out on the top of a stack of paper plates. There were also some stainless-steel knives and forks, the water jug, and three gray enamelware cups ranged in a row. I added some of my sticks to the fire, dropped the rest of the load nearby, and joined Hall on the tarpaulin. Beck came up from the river, drying his hands on a handkerchief. He squatted down beside me.

"Time for a toddy," Hall said. He poured a dollop of whiskey into each of the cups, and then a splash of water from the jug. He passed the cups around and raised his own and smiled. "I like a little toddy about this time of day," he said.

We sat in the sun and drank our drinks. Presently, Hall got up and fed the fire and opened the can of vegetable soup into the pan to heat. Beck followed him with the plate of bass. We would need the cups for the soup, so I gathered them up and rinsed them out in the river. Lying among the pebbles at my feet was a glinting gnarl of what looked like pale-brown sugar. I picked it up and recognized it as a mineral blossom — a fragment of a stalagmite or a stalactite. It was a pretty little thing, and it had an odd velvety feel. I put it in my pocket for a souvenir. When I got back to the camp, the soup was ready. We helped ourselves from the pan and sipped it standing by the fire. The bacon fat had melted in the skillet and was gently simmering. Beck watched it over the rim of his cup as he drank. The fat began to bubble. In a moment, it was seething. Beck put down his cup, picked up the plate of fish, and forked them into the boiling fat. He finished his soup and flipped the fish over and poked the fire — and then they were done. Hall and I were ready with our plates. The bass came out of the skillet with a crisp brown crust, but the meat was white and juicy, and so tender it was falling off the bones. We ate the fish with bread and butter and slices of cheese, and in a silence of total contentment.

By the time we had finished, the coffee was boiling. I got up and rinsed the cups again, and Hall poured out the coffee. Beck opened the can of peaches and passed it around for dessert. We sank into another peaceful silence. But the silence was only ours. An endless stirring of sound lay just beyond it. I listened to the murmur of a distant chute, the splash of a fish, the creak and rustle of the screening trees, the buzz of a frenzy of flies awakened out of season by our fire, and from everywhere came the peeping and piping and faraway calling of birds.

Hall was the first to rouse himself. "I guess we'd better get going," he said. "But, by golly, that was fine. Just great."

"It was a treat," I said.

He looked at me. "You know," he said, "you're probably right. The way things are going these days, it was practically a privilege. I don't know many rivers that you can still count on for your lunch. And a place like this to camp and cook and eat it."

Beck stood up and stretched. "That's for a fact," he said.

We left the gravel bar as clean as we had found it. We buried the cans and burned the paper and smothered the fire with pebbles and sand. As we moved off into the current, I looked back. There was nothing to show that we had been there but a smudge of charring on the two big logs.

The chute I had heard was closer than it sounded. It came tinkling into view just around an elbow bend, and it let us down to the next long pool with one little bump and a gentle splash. The bluff was lower now, and there were boggy patches along its foot. Lizardtail was growing there, and cane bamboo, and a tall, plumed reedlike grass whose name I didn't know.

"That's one of the horsetail family," Hall said, "and about as primitive a plant as you're ever likely to see. It's almost as old as the stone in these limestone bluffs."

"Scouring rush is what I've always heard it called," Beck said. "If you felt it, you'd understand why. It's full of silica. The old people used to use it to scour their pots and pans. I guess they still do."

The bluff continued to dwindle as we moved on down the pool. It fell in less than half a mile from well over a hundred feet to only forty or fifty. Then a break appeared in its face, and it tumbled into a thickly wooded gorge. Through the trees I could see the glint of a winding stream. The bluff reappeared beyond the gorge and climbing steeply, cut away to the left. The river followed it around.

"This is where the Current River starts looking more like a river," Beck said. "That's Jacks Fork coming in there on the right. Jacks Fork doesn't look like much right now, but it carries a lot of water, even at this time of year. You'll see the difference it makes as soon as we get on around the bend. You'll see a different river."

We bobbed past the mouth of Jacks Fork, picked our way through a maze of little islands, and came around the bend. And it was a different river. It was different in every way. It was much wider — half again as wide as before — and deeper and slower. I could only just see the cobbly bottom, and there seemed to be no current at all. Even the bluff looked different. Here and there, the faded gray of its limestone face was pierced by outcroppings of rust-red granite. But there was a current. Beck sat sprawled on his seat, dipping his paddle only to hold our course, but we were moving. The bluff was gray, then red, then faded back to gray again. A huge, peeling sycamore crept slowly up, and slowly crept away. Its branches were hung with clumps of shiny greenery the size of hornet nests. There must have been a dozen of them. I turned and looked again.

"You know what that is," Beck said. "Sure you do. Think of Christmas."

"Mistletoe?" I said.

"That's right," he said. "The woods along the river here are full of it. When I was a kid, we always went out after mistletoe at Christmastime. There were two ways of getting it down. Sometimes you could shinny up the tree and pull a bunch loose. Most of the time, though, it was growing too high up or out too far on the branch to reach. Then we'd shoot it down. We always had a .22 rifle along. We'd hit the branch behind it, and down the bunch would come."

"Pretty good shooting," Hall said.

"Oh, I don't know," Beck said. He gazed up at the trees. "I guess it wasn't quite as easy as it sounds."

We dawdled along for a mile or more. Then the river began to twist and turn. Its banks closed in. Another chute. We scratched down a long, shallow riffle — a mere skin of water drawn over the polished pebbles — and into another lakelike pool. It was even wider than the one above, and, if anything, more sluggish. And it was alive with birds. A downy woodpecker sat raptly listening on the shank of a dying cottonwood. I heard the lovely triplet of a bluebird and saw a flash of red in the brush that could have been a cardinal or a pileated woodpecker's crest. A muttering kingfisher beat low across our bow, and back, and back again — quartering the river like a hound in a field. Six or eight mallards and what looked like a pintail sprang up from a grassy slough and quacked shrilly out of sight. They were

followed from the other shore by a ragged flock of
scaup.

Hall raised an imaginary gun. "Bang!" he said.
He put the gun away and laughed. "I've got a friend
down in Tennessee," he said. "He's a biologist with
the Fish and Wildlife Service, and a fine shot. We
used to go goose-shooting together every fall. That's
good goose country, you know. Well, the last time I
saw him, I mentioned going out again. He was sorry,
he said, but he couldn't. He just couldn't. His particular job these days was working with Canada geese,
and now even the thought of shooting a goose made
him sick. He would almost as soon pull trigger on his
little daughter."

"I can understand that," Beck said.

"Sure," Hall said. "So could I, and I told him so.
I said his feeling was perfectly natural. But what did
he do for sport? Oh, he said, he got his fun. He went
duck-hunting."

The countryside began to change. It lost some of
its rugged look. The woods thinned out on the low
left bank, and a field of stubble corn appeared. At
the end of the field I caught a glimpse of cattle moving among the trees. We passed a landing with a half-
sunken johnboat tied to a willow root. Then we
swung around a bend and the bluff drew back and in
its wake lay a stretch of rolling meadow and a gravel
road leading down to a ferry slip and a little raftlike
ferry. An old man in overalls and a denim jacket was
leaning on the railing. We waved as we passed, and

Beck called out a greeting. The ferryman lifted a benedictional hand.

"Powder Mill Ferry," Hall said. "I guess there must have been a gunpowder mill around here, somewhere back in the old black-powder days. I know there's saltpeter all through these hills. Lee?"

"I reckon so," Beck said. He turned to me. "But don't let that ferry fool you. This isn't the end of the wild. We're going right back in. Powder Mill Ferry is the only crossing between Round Spring, which is well above where we put in, and the bridge down at Van Buren. Van Buren is around thirty-five miles from here. And it's real rough country on both sides of the river almost all the way."

The ferry, the road, and then the meadow drifted out of sight. The bluff moved in again to the water's edge, and the woods above the gravel bar were once more dark and closed with brush. A little green heron flapped across the river. I heard the familiar sound of rushing water. But it wasn't a chute this time. It was a quick little creek, dropping down through the woods and breaking over the gravel bar.

Hall sat up with a start. "Ah," he said. "There it is. I was beginning to think we had missed it. Blue Spring — the prettiest spring on the river. Blue Spring Branch, I should say. The spring itself is back in the woods a ways, but it's worth going up to see. It isn't far. A five-minute walk, at most." He rubbed his hands. "How about it, Lee? Let's put ashore for a minute."

"Suits me," Beck said.

There was a landing just above the mouth of the branch. Hall hopped over the bow and made the boat fast, and I joined him on the beach. Beck lay back in his seat and lit a cigarette.

"You're not coming with us?" I asked.

"Blue Spring's real pretty," he said. "But I've seen it a couple of hundred times. I'd rather just sit here and rest."

I followed Hall across the beach and through an opening in the brush. A sandy path as cramped as a game trail led up a wooded slope. It probably was a game trail. A shiny black animal dropping lay among the leaves. Hall gave it a glance. "Fox," he said.

We emerged into a grassy glade enclosed on two sides by a rocky cliff that rose sheer to treetop height. At the foot of the cliff lay a little round pond of dark-blue water. One bank of the pond was a mossy log and a tumble of stones, and there its quiet waters spilled heavily over and became a plunging creek. The bank where we stopped was gardened with beds of watercress. We stood and gazed at the pond. It was a richer blue than the ocean, or any lake I knew. It was almost a blueberry blue. Hall picked up a white pebble the size of an egg and tossed it into the pond. We watched it sift lazily down through the tinted water and come lightly to rest on the bottom.

"How deep would you say that was?" Hall said.

I hesitated. The pebble looked near enough to reach with a stick, but I remembered how long it had taken to sink. "It must be twenty feet, at least," I said. "Maybe twenty-five."

"It's *fifty*-five," he said. "And it gets deeper back under the cliff. That's where the spring comes up. The reason it's so clear is just that. Spring water is always clear, but deep spring water is the clearest. It contains the least suspended matter."

"It's pretty, all right," I said.

"It is," he said. "And so is that watercress." He squatted down on the bank and reached out and up-rooted a gleaming handful. "I don't know what Wendell's going to give us for supper," he said, "but it's bound to be something good. The least we can do is bring the salad."

When we came down from the spring, the sun had moved behind the bluff and the river was half in shadow. The sky was still an afternoon sky, but it had a shivery look. There was a bite in the air. Hall struggled back into his second flannel shirt and buttoned it up to the neck. Beck had his cap pulled low on his head, and he was wearing gloves. I saw him glance at the sky and then at his watch. As soon as we had shoved off, he shipped his paddle and pushed the uptilted outboard motor down into working position.

"I think we'd better take it the rest of the way with the motor," he said. "We're going to get caught if we don't. Wendell's place is a good six miles from here, and it's getting on toward five." He started the motor, and throttled it down to a heavy throb. "I don't like traveling this river after dark."

We moved off down the river at what felt like breathless speed. After a day of dawdling and drifting, we seemed to be leaping over the water. It wasn't entirely an illusion. I could tell from the rising wind and the mounting wake and the look of the passing shore that we were going fast. But the afternoon was going faster. Even out of the shadow of the bluff and in the fading daylight, it was cold. I looked at my watch. It was twenty minutes to six. I hunched down in my jacket and watched Hall hunching down in his two red shirts and his windproof pants, and listened to the river slipping and slapping at the boat.

There was a sudden silence, and we were suddenly drifting again. Beck had cut the motor. "Here we are," he said. His voice sounded small and tired. He tilted the outboard clear of the water and picked up the paddle. We crawled over a shoal and alongside a catwalk pier. Beyond the pier was a rising slope of open woods, and at the top of the rise sat a white stone house with a row of lighted windows and a big stone chimney plumed with a wisp of woodsmoke. I stepped up onto the pier, and in the darkening sky beyond the house hung a moon as thin as a hair. It was a winter moon. It looked as cold and as blue as the farthest star.

The Last of the Keys

When a man despoils a work of art we call him a
vandal, when he despoils a work of nature we call
him a developer.

— JOSEPH WOOD KRUTCH

▲▲▲

ELLIOTT KEY and its several smaller neighbors —
Sands Key, Totten Key, Old Rhodes Key,
Porgy Key, Adams Key, Reid Key, Meigs Key, the
Rubicon Keys, and Caesar's Rock — are a string of
densely wooded coral islands, lying some eight or
nine miles off the southeastern coast of Florida, at
the mouth of Biscayne Bay. They are among the
northernmost of the Florida keys, and the only ones
of any size that are accessible solely by boat. They
are also the only ones of any size that have so far
escaped development. They are roadless, waterless,
and practically uninhabited. It is the hope of many
people in Florida and elsewhere that these little islands may remain unspoiled, and this hope is shared
by the Department of the Interior. The department
has proposed* that they be acquired and preserved

* The proposal after much opposition was finally approved by
Congress, and the Islandia keys were incorporated into the National
Park System as the Biscayne National Monument in 1968.

47

for public enjoyment as a national monument — Islandia National Monument.

I had my first glimpse of the Islandia keys from a National Park Service launch. It was around eight o'clock on a bright, blue April morning in 1964, and we were crawling down a canal that starts near the mainland town of Homestead and leads eastward into Biscayne Bay. My companions were a young Everglades National Park ranger named George Schesventer; a fishery biologist named Richard K. Robinson, from the United States Fish and Wildlife Service office at Vero Beach; and a National Park Service landscape architect named Robert L. Steenhagen. Steenhagen, like me, was a visitor to Florida; his office was in Philadelphia. He sat alone in the stern of the boat in the shade of a big, floppy planter's hat. Robinson and I stood forward with Schesventer, who was at the wheel. Far away across the shining waters of the bay, a dark-green line lay along the faded-blue horizon.

"That's it," Schesventer told me. "That's Islandia. Most of what you see — all that line of land straight ahead is Elliott Key. Don't let it fool you, though. It looks a lot bigger than it is. Elliott Key is a good seven miles long, but you can walk across it in about five minutes. I doubt if it's half a mile wide. Still, compared to the others, it's huge. It's five times the size of Sands Key or Totten Key, and at least ten times the size of Porgy and Reid and the rest. It's a hundred times the size of Caesar's Rock."

"Caesar's Rock doesn't have to be big," Robinson said. "It's famous. You've heard of Edward Teach — the pirate they called Blackbeard. Well, his chief lieutenant was a Negro named Caesar — or Black Caesar — and Caesar's Rock is where he used to careen his ship when it needed repairs. There's a rock ledge there, and he sank a couple of iron rings in it to run his lines through. I understand they've got the rings in a museum around here somewhere."

"Elliott Key has some history, too," Schesventer said. "They tell me Audubon stopped off there on his trip from St. Augustine to Dry Tortugas. And General John C. Breckinridge, the Confederate Secretary of War, is supposed to have hidden out there on his flight to Cuba after Appomattox. Some people say he had what was left of the Confederate treasury with him."

"Some people say there's treasure on Caesar's Rock," Robinson said.

We emerged from the canal into Biscayne Bay and made our way down an avenue of channel stakes. On each of the stakes sat a bird. Most of the birds were big black cormorants. The others were big royal terns. They opened their wings and jumped listlessly into the air as we passed, and then dropped listlessly back on the stakes. Schesventer increased the throttle. The bow came up, the wake fanned out,

49

and the launch took a giant step. Steenhagen grabbed his hat. We cleared the channel in a rush of wind, and the water turned a blinding turquoise green.

"I thought we'd start with Sands Key," Schesventer said. "That's it coming up on the left. It looks like just more of Elliott Key, but they're separated by a little pass. Sands Cut, they call it. We'll see it in a minute or two. Sands Key is real interesting. It's got one of the few good stands of big mahogany left on the keys, and it's got the only sandy ocean beach."

"Is that why they call it Sands Key?" I said.

"I wouldn't be surprised," he said.

"I would," Robinson said. " 'Sands' is a corruption of 'Saunders.' A family named Saunders owned it originally. It's the same with Elliott Key. I mean, its name is another corruption. The old maps list it as Ellicott Key."

"Is that right?" Schesventer said. "That's real interesting, Dick. It really is."

A break appeared in the wall of greenery ahead. It broadened into a corridor of bright-blue water leading to the ocean. Schesventer gave the wheel a turn, and we headed north. Sands Cut shrank and disappeared, and Sands Key began to take shape. The wall of greenery became individual trees, and the trees became mangroves, their centipede trunks standing knee-deep in the waters of the bay. There was no beach. All the trees along the shore were mangroves, but here and there in the distance was the dome of a big mahogany or the feathery spire of an

Australian pine. Steenhagen came up from the stern.

"Look at all that Australian pine," he said. "I didn't know it had spread to the keys. That's a heck of a note."

"It's practically everywhere," Schesventer said.

"We'll have to get rid of it," Steenhagen said. "It doesn't belong on these keys, and we don't want it. We don't want exotics here. We want to preserve the indigenous flora. That's the whole point of the Monument."

"I agree," Schesventer said. "It's a nuisance, all right. But the funny thing is it's really not a bad tree. It's a hardwood tree and it grows fast and it's pretty to look at. The only trouble is that it spreads. They tell me it started with a handful of seeds that somebody brought in from Australia in a Bull Durham tobacco sack about forty years ago. It took over like a weed. There must have been a niche just waiting for it."

"Actually, it isn't even a pine," Robinson said. "It's a variety of casuarina — what they call 'willow' on the Carribean islands."

We rounded a point, and a narrow inlet came into view. Schesventer eased the throttle. We crept into the mouth of the inlet and under a canopy of mangroves. It was dark beneath the arching trees, and breathlessly hot, and the only sound was the muffled rumble of the engine. After fifty yards or so, the inlet widened and became a marshy cove. Mangrove thickets lined its shores, but there were occasional cavelike clearings among the trees, and at one of the clearings stood a little platform pier. The sun came blazing back, and the air was hotter and heavier than ever. There was a sudden flash of white across the water. It was a big white bird with trailing yellow legs and a six-foot spread of wings. It flapped away behind a screen of trees.

"Hoo!" Schesventer said. "How about that? A great white heron! Audubon's great white heron! I call that quite a sight. You very seldom see one of those fellows anywhere but around these lonely keys. They nest in the mangroves."

"I don't plan to touch the mangroves," Steenhagen said.

Schesventer brought the launch alongside the pier. We made fast and climbed ashore. A gravelly path of gray fossil coral led up through the crowding mangroves toward the ocean. Robinson took the lead, and we followed him into a sweltering twilight. For a moment, it was like being back in the inlet. Then, thirty or forty yards from the pier, the mangroves thinned and petered out. In their place was a hardwood jungle — mahogany, Australian pine, buttonwood, lignum vitae, and a handsome tree with pale-gray bark and shiny green leaves that I had never seen before.

"That's another native of the keys," Schesventer said. "You find it only here and on the Caribbean islands. They call it a white stopper. It's got a smell at certain seasons that can stop you in your tracks. Which is how it got its name, I guess."

"It smells like a skunk," Robinson said.

"That's right," Schesventer said. "It does. But the interesting thing is the *fact* of this stand of hardwoods. It's a perfect lesson in ecology. The reason these trees are growing here is a little hummock that forms the spine of the island. It gives them a possible environment. I doubt whether the elevation here is much more than a foot above that back there at the pier, but those few inches make a world of difference."

"They make a different world," Robinson said. "And so would almost any development of these keys. That's what we want to avoid. That's the one big reason for the Monument."

"The only development I plan is to keep things just the way they are," Steenhagen said. "Except, of course, for those Australian pines."

There was a dazzle of sunlight up ahead. The hardwood jungle ended, the path dropped down through a sea-grape thicket, and we came out onto a narrow strip of chalky shell-sand beach. We stood and looked at the ocean. It was as calm and blue and empty as the sky. A steady breeze came off the water. I could feel the sweat of the cove and the jungle drying on my face. Steenhagen took off his planter's hat and gave a grunt of satisfaction.

Robinson lighted a cigarette. "Well," he said, "where do we go from here?"

53

"How about down to the Cut?" Schesventer said. "It's only about a mile."

"I'd like to see the Cut," Steenhagen said.

We moved off through the powdery sand. It was intensely white in the glare of the sun, and it had the feel underfoot of dust. The beach it formed wasn't much of a bathing beach. From the puddles at the waterline to the brushy banks of the jungle, it was hardly the width of a sidewalk, and it was strewn with seaborne litter. But it made a wonderful walk. We picked our way over waterlogged planks and coconut husks and coral shards and barkless logs and lobster buoys and seaweed wreaths and fish skeletons and tattered sponges and snakes of tarry rope and conch shells and the purple sausage balloons of Portuguese men-of-war. Schesventer stopped and bent over.

"Remember those old drawings of Robinson Crusoe in his pointed cap?" he said. "This is what I've always figured he wore." He held up a shaggy conical sponge. "All he had to do was shop around until he found one that fitted. I thought we might do some snorkeling after lunch. You'll see plenty of it growing then." He hung the sponge on an overhanging branch. "Basket sponge is what they call it."

"This beach is full of interesting loot," Robinson said. "You can find things here from all over the world. Like this." He touched with his toe the still recognizable remains of a white birch sapling. "Or this." He picked up a big round seed that looked like a flattened horse chestnut.

"What is it?" I asked.

"It's one of the giant tropical beans," he said, and rubbed it briskly on his thigh. It shone like polished mahogany. "It's called a snuffbox bean. It grows all over northern South America. I've never seen it growing, but they say it's quite a sight. It grows on a climbing vine in seed pods three or four feet long."

"What about Indian artifacts?" Steenhagen asked.

"I dug up a sliver of bone along here once," Robinson said. "Somebody said it looked like Arawak work."

"There's an artifact for you," Schesventer said. He pointed to a flotsam bottle in the sand. It was made of green plastic and had white lettering across the face: "Mennen Spray Deodorant." He gave it a kick. "I don't think it's Arawak. It looks more like the work of the Miami tribe."

The brushy beach bank flattened out, and a tongue of mangroves ran down to the water's edge. The curious calmness of the ocean here was plainly permanent. The mangroves could never have established themselves on a stretch of beach that was repeatedly scoured by surf. There would be a protective reef not far offshore. We left the beach and cut inland over a thick carpet of rubbery saltwort. The trade-wind breeze dwindled and died away. In the lee of the mangroves was a gravelly meadow bristling with prickly pear and dildo cactus and monstrous century plants. Some of the century plants were thirty feet high, and with their armor of green and reddish scales, they had a stark, unearthly aspect. They looked like giant stalks of asparagus. There was a rustling at the edge of the jungle, and a boat-tailed grackle sailed out of the trees. Schesventer; spun around.

"There he goes," he said. "Look at him go!"

"Who?" I said. "That grackle?"

"No," he said. "No. Over there, in that gumbo-limbo tree. That black squirrel. He's heading down that bottom branch."

I thought I saw a shadowy movement. Then it was gone. There was a distant rustle of leaves.

"Did you see him?" Schesventer asked.

"I got a glimpse," I said.

"Too bad," he said. "That was another specialty of these keys. Man, he was a beauty! And a big one, too. If you didn't know, you could almost have taken him for a big black cat."

We came out on the beach again. The breeze returned, but not for long. Our way was soon blocked by another clump of oceanic mangroves, and behind the mangroves was another sweltering meadow. At the end of the meadow, framed in jungle greenery, was the bright-blue water of Sands Cut. The Sands Key beach along the Cut was a spit of rough-and-tumble coral. On Elliott Key, a hundred yards or so across the water, there was only a wall of mangroves. We walked out on the spit. The rocks at the end of the spit were overgrown with bright-colored snails and barnacles. Ahead of us, the bottom shelved off steeply, but the water was very clear, and I could see turtle grass growing there. A pair of silver mullet were browsing through the waving grass.

"Pretty, isn't it?" Schesventer said.

"It's beautiful," Steenhagen said.

"It makes a nice walk," Robinson said. "The only trouble is, it's the end of the line. We've got to go back the way we came. You can't get through on the bay side. That part of the island is nothing but jungle and swamp." He lighted a cigarette. "I don't mean we couldn't possibly get through," he said. "I guess we could if we had to. The conquistadors did — and in full armor. I often think of those old Spaniards when I see primitive jungle like this. I think of them sweating inside that heavy armor and hacking their way through these swamps. It gives you the creeps."

"It does for a fact," Schesventer said.

Robinson pitched his cigarette into the water. "Let's get back to the boat," he said. "I'm getting hungry."

We walked back along the beach and down the path to the boat. After the oean breeze, the jungle and the cove seemed hotter than ever. There was no sign of the great white heron. Schesventer started the engine, and we moved across the cove and out of the inlet into the open water of the bay. We turned south. I stood in the breeze of the boat and watched the mangrove coast go by, and then Sands Cut. Then we were moving down the identical mangrove coast of Elliott Key. Schesventer looked at his watch.

"Twenty minutes to twelve," he said. "I'm getting hungry, too. Dade County has a little park and a small-boat anchorage about halfway along this side of Elliott Key. I thought we'd put in there for lunch. They don't have any drinking water, but the caretaker generally has some soda on ice, and it's nice sitting under the trees."

"I'm interested in that anchorage," Steenhagen said. "It sounds like a natural for us. My idea would be to make it the only entrance to the Monument. The only regular entrance, anyway."

"One entrance is plenty," Robinson said. He touched Schesventer on the shoulder. "Wait a minute, George. Slow down. I think I see something interesting. Just off to the right there. It looks like a bunch of sargassum weed."

"I think you're right," Schesventer said.

He slowed the throttle and gave the wheel a turn. The launch slumped down to a crawl. Robinson leaned over the gunwale and came up with a dripping cluster of bulbous brown leaves and yellow berrylike floats.

"This is the alga that forms the Sargasso Sea," he said. "I mean, it ends up there. It grows on the

rocks along the coast down here and in the West In-
dies until a storm comes along and tears it loose.
Then it floats away on the Gulf Stream. But the interesting thing is the animal life it supports. Even a
little bunch like this can be a whole ecology."

He gave the seaweed a twist and a shake, and a
puddle of water spread across the deck. It teemed
with tiny creatures. We squatted down around the
puddle. There were pea-sized crabs and inch-long
shrimp and half-inch shrimp and eighth-of-an-inch
shrimp and crustaceans no bigger than grains of
sand. The shrimp and the crustaceans were transpar-
ent. They looked gray against the gray of the deck.
The crabs were brown and yellow — the colors of
the weed. Schesventer turned back to the wheel. Robinson gathered up the crabs and the larger shrimp
and tossed them overboard. He tossed the seaweed
after them, and wiped his hands on his trousers.

"You'd be surprised how fast those things can
stink up a boat," he said.

The anchorage on Elliott Key was the lee of a
point of land enclosed by a dogleg jetty made of
coral rock. Part of the jetty had been surfaced, to
serve as a landing wharf. There was a navigational
light and marker at the end of the jetty and boldly
printed sign: NO DOGS ALLOWED. A brown pelican
was perched on top of the sign. It paid no attention
to us. Two low white buildings faced the anchorage
from a rough clearing. Around the clearing rose the

jungle. We docked at the wharf near a battered cabin cruiser with trolling masts and a fighting chair. It was the only other boat in the anchorage. We walked up the wharf to a picnic table and two long benches in the shade of a big sapodilla tree. Robinson had our lunch in a brown paper bag. He spread it out on the table — cold baked beans, hard-boiled eggs, rat-trap cheese, and crackers. Schesventer went on to one of the buildings and came back with four bottles of cold root beer. We sat in the shade and ate our lunch and drank the root beer and watched the pelican dive for fish. It took off from the sign and soared, and then dived with its wings still spread. It hit the water with a tremendous splash and explosion. Robinson finished the last of his root beer and lighted a cigarette.

"You know something?" he said. "I'm still hungry."

"So am I," Schesventer said. "I'd like some dessert, and I think I know where there is some."

"Where?" Robinson asked.

"Follow me."

"Oh, you mean fruit," Robinson said. "That's a good idea."

I collected the empty bottles and the remains of our lunch and carried them over to a trash can at the foot of the wharf. A gray-haired woman came out on the deck of the cabin cruiser and watched me. She was chewing gum. I rejoined the others, and

Schesventer led the way across the grass and across a field of beach morning glories and onto a jungle track. It was as still and dim and hot as the path through the Sands Key jungle. Nothing moved, and nothing came into sight. After about a mile, the jungle opened up and the track petered out. We emerged into a sunny little savanna. It was strewn with gray coral boulders, and among the boulders were patches of grass and scattered clumps of trees. Most of the trees were key lime trees, hung with tiny yellow fruit, but there were also several brilliantly fruited orange trees. Schesventer stopped and picked a couple of oranges. Then he moved on to what looked like a palm of some sort. It was a small tree with a long, slender trunk and a shaggy crown of big, starlike leaves, and just under the crown was a cluster of yellow fruit about the size and shape of eggplant. Schesventer looked at me, and then at Steenhagen, and then back at me again.

"You don't know what this is?" he said. "It's a papaya. Here — hold these a minute." He handed me the oranges, and turned and shinnied up the tree. He got a grip on a branch and tore loose three papayas. "Catch," he said, and let the papayas drop. Robinson caught two of them, and Steenhagen caught the other. He gave it a doubtful look.

"I think maybe I'll just have an orange," he said.

Schesventer slid back to the ground. "I wouldn't recommend it," he said. "These oranges here aren't regular oranges. They're wild oranges, and they're almost as sour as a lemon. I picked them to eat with the papayas. They go real good together."

He sat down on a boulder with a papaya and one of the oranges, and opened a horn-handled clasp knife. He quartered the orange and set the pieces aside. Then he skinned the papaya. The fruit beneath the heavy skin was the golden yellow of a ripe muskmelon. He cut the papaya into slices and passed them around and squeezed a few drops of orange juice on each. Steenhagen took a cautious bite of his slice.

"Not bad," he said.

"It's delicious," Schesventer said.

It *was* delicious. The papaya itself had no more flavor than an oyster, but it was soft and juicy and warm from the sun, and its blandness softened the bite of the bitter orange and gave it a curious tang. It tasted like nothing I had ever eaten before.

Schesventer skinned another papaya and stuck his knife in the fruit. "Help yourself when you're ready," he said, and stood up. "I'm going to pick a few limes for my wife. She's crazy about key-lime pie."

When we got back to the boat, the cabin cruiser was gone. So was the pelican. The only sign of life in the park was a little palm warbler scratching for food near the picnic table. We shoved off from the wharf and moved across the empty anchorage and around the jetty and headed down the mangrove coast. I found a seat in the stern and sat back with the breeze in my face. The mangrove coast ran on ahead as far as I could see. Robinson said something to Schesventer and squatted down behind the windshield and opened a locker drawer. He brought out four snorkel masks and four pairs of rubber flippers. Then he came back and dropped down on the seat beside me.

"How do you feel about some snorkeling?" he said. "We thought we'd put in just below that big point up ahead."

"I'd like it," I said.

"Good," he said. "I guarantee you'll like it here. There's more to the Monument than just these keys, you know. It also includes the waters around them. In my opinion, the water is at least as important as the land — particularly the water here on the bay side. It supports some of the prettiest marine gardens I've ever seen or ever hope to see. The prettiest and the biggest. They cover hundreds of acres. They run all the way from Sands Key down to Totten. And they're accessible. That's the unusual thing. The water all along this coast is only three or four feet deep for almost a mile offshore. Anybody can enjoy them — even kids. All you need is a snorkel. I'd hate to see anything happen to these gardens. They're largely why I'm so strong for the Monument. The only way to keep the gardens is to keep the keys unspoiled. You know how development works. It never

63

leaves well enough alone. Even the most enlightened developer would want to clear and drain and fill and probably even bulkhead the mangrove swamps, and that, of course, would be the end of the gardens. Marine life depends in large part for its existence on coastal swamps and marshes. That's where a lot of the nutrients that feed and fertilize it originate. They flow out with every tide."

We came around the point and into a kind of bay. Six little cattle egrets rose up from an outpost mangrove and drifted down the shore and vanished among the trees. We moved slowly across the glassy blue water. It began to look very shallow. Schesventer beckoned Robinson and me forward. Relieved of our weight, the stern lifted a little, and the boat moved safely on for another fifty feet. Then Schesventer gave a grunt and cut the engine, and Steenhagen threw over the anchor. We were still almost a hundred yards from shore. I looked over the gunwale. We had anchored over a meadow of turtle grass, and I could see the long green blades bending like corn in a sudden breath of submarine breeze. Sponges grew among the clumps of grass. There were basket sponges like the one on the Sands Key beach, and big brown loggerhead sponges, two or three feet high, and, here and there, growing flat on the bottom, a flaming-scarlet fire sponge. I didn't see any fish or any turtles. The boat had probably frightened them away.

We changed into swimming trunks, and Robinson handed out the snorkel masks and the flippers. Schesventer hung a ladder over the side. I was the last to go down. The water came to about my thighs, and it was almost as warm as the air. It had a heavy, salty feel. I stood ankle-deep in velvety grass and gazed around. The others were drifting like logs toward the mangrove thickets along the shore. I pulled down my mask and sank into the water — and there was Robinson's garden. The grass and the sponges I had seen from the boat were only its shrubs and trees. Its flowers were corals and algae. I floated over a bed of tiny tulips. They were creamy white, with delicate pale-green stripes, and even in underwater magnification they looked no bigger than the blossoms of babies'-breath. Beyond the tulips was a spray of white coral fingers hung with pink and yellow sequins. The sifted light gave everything a silvery, moonlit clarity. A fire sponge blazed up ahead. I paddled gently toward it, and something moved at its edge. I recognized the stemmed eyes and the long antennae of a spiny lobster. It backed stealthily under the scarlet sponge.

A shadow fell across the water. I had reached the edge of the mangroves. A school of glass minnows burst around a clump of grass and disappeared in the sudden twilight. I stopped paddling and waited, and after a moment the twilight seemed to brighten. There were dim shafts of light in the distance. I moved on a little farther and peered in among the dangling mangrove roots and the rooted

65

mangrove trunks. The roots and trunks were hung with barnacles and hairy moss and shiny creepers of algae, and the aisles between them were alive with fish. There were big spotted groupers. There were blue parrot fish and yellow parrot fish and green parrot fish. There were gray sailor's-choice, and gray French grunts with bright-red mouths and yellow fins. There were schools of fat mojarra and fingerling herring and foot-long mangrove snappers. They swam up to my mask and under my arms and down my back. I lay there and watched their comings and goings, and I had never seen anything so lovely. It was so lovely that I felt suddenly angry — angry at a possibility. I knew I would probably never visit these gardens again, but the thought that they might not always be here to be seen — that the effort to preserve them might fail — filled me with a kind of rage.

Ricing

THE ROAD climbed up through the spruce and aspen woods to the top of another rise, and below was another creek in a cloud of morning mist, and another wooden bridge across it, and, off to the left, another glimpse of the lake. A car was parked on the far side of the bridge, and an Indian in a baseball cap was leaning against the hood. He watched us come bumping down the hill. There were three of us in a Chevrolet pickup truck, with an aluminum canoe in back, and the lake was Lower Rice Lake, in the White Earth Chippewa Indian Reservation in northwestern Minnesota. My companions were Charles Bullard, assistant area forester for the Minneapolis area office of the Bureau of Indian Affairs, and Richard Sheehan, a special consultant to the Minneapolis office on public information, and we had come up to the White Earth Reservation to see the opening of the wild-rice harvest. The Indian meant that this was the place we were looking for. He was a tribal-council ricing warden.

We crossed the bridge in a rumble of planks and pulled up at the warden's car. The warden was a big man with a heavy face, and he wore a silver badge: SPECIAL POLICE. He looked at the truck and then into the cab — at Bullard at the wheel, and then at Sheehan, and then at me. Only Indians were permitted to rice on Lower Rice Lake, and we weren't Indians.

"It's O.K., Warden," Bullard said. "We're not ricing. I'm with the B.I.A. We just came up to look at the crop."

The warden nodded.

"Where do we go?" Bullard said. "Where are they going to put in?"

The warden looked at him. "Bungo's Landing," he said.

"And where is that?"

"First left."

"Thank you, Warden," Bullard said, and put the truck in gear.

We moved off down the road.

"What was he so sour about?" I said.

Sheehan laughed.

"About being a warden on opening day," Bullard said. "He'd rather be out ricing."

The way to Bungo's Landing was a rutted lane. A few yards down the lane lay the lump of a run-over porcupine. The lane wound for half a mile through scraping brush to a grassy clearing filled with thirty or forty parked cars. Most of the cars were dusty old Fords or Chevrolets with dented fenders and big tail fins, and all of them had canoe racks fixed to their tops. A narrow track led down from the clearing through more brush and a cattail marsh to an old log pier and a confusion of Indians and canoes. There were men and women in the crowd, and boys and girls, and even a few small children. Beyond the pier was a stretch of open water, and beyond the open water was a great expanse of green that looked like a field of ripening wheat. It spread away a mile or more across the lake to the wooded eastern shore and off to the north and south as far as I could see. That was the rice.

We drove through the clearing and down the track to the edge of the pier, and Bullard backed the truck around and Sheehan and I got out and unloaded the canoe. Some of the Indians turned and watched us, and one of them came over to the truck. He was eating a candy bar, and he had a warden's badge on his jacket. Bullard seemed to know him.

"How does it look?" Bullard said.

"It looks real good," the warden said. "It looks so good the council had me here on watch all night. Some of these guys, you'd be surprised how they try to get out there ricing ahead of time."

Bullard smiled. "They say night ricing is always the best," he said.

"I know they do," the warden said. "And it's true. The rice falls better at night. The dew and the damp seems to loosen up the heads. That don't make it legal, though."

"No," Bullard said. He gazed at the lake. "It's going to be breezy out there," he said.

"I know it is," the warden said. "I only hope it don't get up and really blow — not before noon, anyway. We stop at noon today. A lot of the heads are just about ready to shatter. A good hard wind could lose us a lot of rice." He finished his candy bar and wiped his hands on his pants. "I better get back to my boat. It's almost time to start."

"Are you ricing, too?" Bullard said.

The warden laughed. "I didn't stand around here all last night for nothing," he said. He laughed again and turned away.

"We'd better get going ourselves," Sheehan said.

"All right," Bullard said. "Just as soon as I get rid of this truck."

Bullard headed the truck back up the track to the clearing, and Sheehan and I carried the canoe out to the sagging end of the pier and slid it into the water. Then we went back and got our lunch and the paddles and the pole. The pole was for moving through the rice. It was twenty feet long, with two metal duckbill plates the size of hands flared out on hinges at one end. Wild-rice lakes are very shallow, but they have soft bottoms of mucky peat that is often six or eight feet deep, and the duckbills on the canoe pole

72

were to give it a purchase in the muck. The Indians were all on the water now, and waiting. There were two Indians in each canoe. One stood with a pole in the stern, and the other sat on the center thwart with a pair of wooden drumstick flails. The Indian with the flails was the ricer. Most of the ricing teams were men, but there were also men and women, boys and girls, mothers and sons, and even pairs of girls. The only Indians left on the pier were four little boys. One of the boys was as blond as a Swede. I looked for the warden and found him in a canoe with a tall man in glasses slouching on a pole in the stern. Back in the woods I could hear a woodpecker knocking. The sky overhead was high and clear and very blue, and the sun was beginning to warm. It was going to be a sparkling day. The warden raised his hand. The polers gave a heave and the canoes began to move. I looked at my watch. It was exactly nine o'clock.

Bullard was right about the breeze. It was a gusty breeze blowing out of the south, and we felt it as soon as we left the pier. Sheehan was poling, and Bullard and I had the paddles, and the three of us had to work to make it across the open water against the broadside breeze. I was sweating when we finally yawed into the shelter of the standing rice. One of the ricing canoes had come this way, and we moved into the rice along its bent and broken trail. There was no sign of the boat itself. It could have been anywhere in the acres of rice up ahead. There was no sign of any of the ricers. There was nothing but water and rice and sky. The rice stood three or four feet above the water, and the water was brown but clear, with a glint of yellow light, and I could clearly see the reedlike stalks emerging from the bottom muck a couple of feet below. The rice was less dense than it looked to be from the shore. There were thick stands and thin stands and sudden little openings where no rice grew at all. But even the thinnest stands were too thick for paddling, and I was glad to sit back and let Sheehan push us along with his pole.

So was Bullard. He lighted a cigarette and looked up at the passing rice. That was what he was here for. The White Earth Reservation is one of the biggest reservations in Minnesota, and wild rice from the many reservation lakes is the main cash crop of the Indians. Bullard broke off a hanging head of rice and held it out — eight tight inches of green-hulled grains ripening into purple at the top of the cluster. "I call that good-looking rice," he said.

"It doesn't look a lot like rice," I said. "It looks more like wheat or oats."

"I know what you mean," he said. "As a matter of fact, wild rice isn't really a rice. I mean, it isn't related to cultivated rice. They're entirely different plants."

"They're entirely different genera," Sheehan said. "Cultivated rice is *Oryza sativa*. Wild rice is *Zizania aquatica*."

Bullard tossed the *Zizania aquatica* head away.

"The only thing they have in common is they're both aquatic grasses that produce an edible seed," he said. "It was the white man that started calling this stuff wild rice. I guess because he found it growing in water. The Indian word for it means 'good berry.' "

"They called it *manomin*," Sheehan said. *"Manomin* is the Indian name." He rested on his pole. "Do you want to keep on this way? There's another boat off there to the left. I can see the top of the pole."

"This way is O.K.," Bullard said.

Sheehan bent back to work, and we moved on through a heavy stand of rice. He knew how to use the pole. I sat and watched him. He didn't drive the canoe along by might and main. He eased it along by thrusting the pole into the water with his hands near the middle of the shaft and then walking them up to the top. I turned back to the trail ahead. The rice we were passing through now was the tallest rice I had seen. Some of the stalks were five feet high. And it was alive with little tan moths. They were on the rice and in the air and fluttering on the skin of the water in a wild, end-of-summer excitement. The stand began to thin, and a pondlike opening appeared. There was a clash and clatter of wings. Seven little ducks sprang up together from the open water and rocketed away across the rice. They were teal — blue-winged teal. I could see their bright wing patches shining in the sun like a mirror reflection of the sky.

75

"They like wild rice, too," Bullard said. "They depend on it. At this time of year, it's probably the main food of teal and wood duck and mallards and the other puddle ducks. It's also important to some of the shorebirds, and even to songbirds like rusty blackbirds and bobolinks and redwings. And the birds get their share of the crop. They get as much as the Indians do."

"How much is that?" I said.

"About ten per cent," he said.

"Ten per cent?" I said. "The Indians only get ten per cent of the crop? What happens to the rest of it?"

"It goes into the lake," he said. "It either shatters in the wind or the ricers accidentally knock it into the water. The Indian way of ricing isn't very efficient. They lose ten times as much as they get. Look at the amount of rice the boat alone breaks down. But a lot of people say it's still the best way. They say the rice that's lost isn't wasted. It not only feeds the ducks — it seeds the next year's crop."

"It's also the only legal way," Sheehan said. "The use of any kind of mechanical harvester on the Indian lakes and public waters is prohibited by law in Minnesota, and there are similar laws in Wisconsin and the Canadian wild-rice provinces. But Minnesota has the strictest regulations, and it's the one that matters most. It produces almost ninety per cent of the total wild-rice crop."

"The ricing law is based on tradition," Bullard said. "Indian tradition. It's the way the Indians want it. Mechanical harvesters have been used on private paddies for years. They work like a kind of combine on pontoons. They take two or three times as much rice as the traditional way, and if the operators know their job they can be quite selective. They can be every bit as selective as the best hand ricer. I mean, they can harvest just the ripened hulls and leave the rest of the head for later, when it's ripe. And they seem to leave plenty of rice for seeding. I'm not so sure how much they leave for the ducks. I do know this. They'd be a lot more efficient if wild rice wasn't wild — if it was like a cultivated grain and had a firm head that didn't shatter as it ripened. Wild rice is a complicated problem. But I think we'll keep on ricing by hand until somebody perfects a non-shattering strain of rice."

"It must be about the last hand industry left," I said.

"I wouldn't be surprised," he said.

Sheehan was looking off across the fields of blowing rice. "There's a boat just up ahead," he said.

The boat was the boat whose trail we were following. It was a homemade wooden ricing boat with a woman ricer and with a teen-age boy in dark glasses at the pole. The woman had on a red hunting cap and a man's blue denim shirt worn backward and buttoned up the back to keep out the itchy chaff. As we came up behind them, they looked around. Ricers usually keep their distance. The woman and the boy looked startled, and then impassive.

Bullard smiled and raised a friendly hand. "We're not ricing," he said. "I'm with the B.I.A. We're just looking around."

"Hi," the woman said.

The boy said nothing.

"What do you think of the rice this year?" Bullard said.

"Pretty good," the woman said.

The boy shoved hard on his pole. The boat moved on and away, and the woman took up her flails. She caught four or five stalks of rice with her right-hand flail and pressed them over the gunwale of the canoe and tapped the gathered heads with the other flail. The ripe purple hulls and some of the green hulls shattered away from the heads and fell into a soggy green heap of hulls and stems at her feet. Then she turned and gathered together a cluster of stalks on the other side of the boat and tapped the heads, and another shatter of hulls dropped into the heap. I watched her swing back to the passing rice on the other side. She moved with grace, but it didn't look like easy work.

Bullard was watching her, too. He made a wry face. "Well," he said. "She's only got till noon." He sat back. "O.K., Dick. Let's go find that other boat you saw."

We let the woman and the boy pull away. Then

we left their trail and cut into an unbroken stand of rice. The moths were everywhere here. We crossed another patch of open water. It was patterned with lily pads like a garden pond. The rice closed in again. Sheehan pushed us along between the overhanging stalks. Most of the heads were dead ripe, and they shattered at the touch of the boat. The scratchy hulls blew in my face and down my neck. The woman ricer had the right idea with her shirt buttoned up the back. We began to gather a litter of shattered rice. I stirred the litter with my foot. There were fallen moths mixed in with the rice.

"I see what they mean about shattering," I said. "We're going to have some rice by the time we go in."

"We should have bought a license," Bullard said.

"You know something?" Sheehan said. "That breeze is picking up. I can feel the difference in the way the boat handles. Even in this real thick rice."

"You want to take a break?" Bullard said.

"I wouldn't mind a cup of coffee," Sheehan said.

The lunch bag with the coffee was stowed under my seat. I twisted around and bent over — and the boat gave a lurch. Sheehan jabbed with his pole, and the boat settled back. "Hey," he said. "Watch it." He sat carefully down and carefully laid the long pole away. "You're in a canoe."

Bullard laughed, but I only nodded. I was thinking what it would feel like to fall into that bottomless muck. It would be a long, slimy crawl back to the pier. Moving gingerly, I reached for the lunch bag again, and got out the coffee. It was in a Thermos bottle with three cap cups. I poured the coffee and passed two cups to Bullard, and he passed one on to Sheehan.

Bullard took a drink of his coffee and laughed again.

"That reminded me of a dog I had one time," he said. "My wife and I were out duckhunting in a canoe like this, and we had this young dog along. She was a brown Lab. We were sitting out there in the middle of the river, and a flight of mallards came over. I got my gun up and shot one, and he came tumbling down, and the dog gave a jump to retrieve him — and over we all went. But I'd trained my wife pretty well. She remembered to hold her gun clear. She held it over her head when she went under, and then came up and waded to shore and never got a drop of water on it."

"Oh, boy," Sheehan said. "Where was that, Chuck?"

"It was on the Mississippi," Bullard said.

"The Mississippi?" I said. I stared at him. I knew something about the Mississippi. I had lived in St. Louis. It wasn't a river that you could wade across. "Your wife waded to shore from the middle of the Mississippi River?"

"What?" Bullard said. "Oh. This wasn't the Mississippi River you're thinking about. This was

here in Minnesota — just south of where the river
rises. The Mississippi where we were hunting isn't
much more than a stream."

It was around ten-thirty when we finished our
coffee. The ricing day was half over. We moved on
through dense, unbroken rice, with the sun high and
bright overhead. It had been unmistakably autumn
driving up to the lake in the frosty early morning,
but now it was almost summer again. Down in the
rice and out of the breeze it was hot. We were still
deep in the heavy rice when we found the ricers we
were looking for. The breeze brought us the sound
of their voices, and we heard them before we saw
them. They sounded like girls, and they were — two
girls in their middle twenties. They watched us come
up, and the ricer smiled and waved. She was a short,
fat girl with dark-red hair. The other girl had her
hair tied up in a black net scarf, and she wore rhine-
stone glasses and a big blue sweatshirt. She looked at
Bullard. "You're the B.I.A. man," she said.
    "That's right," he said. "How's the rice?"
    "Oh, it's good," she said.
    The ricer put down her flails and lighted a ciga-
rette. "We've been out three days," she said. "We've
been on Hay Creek and down on Mud Lake. But this
is the best rice we've seen."
    "And, thank goodness, no worms," the other girl
said. "I hate those worms. They bite."

"Rice worms?" Sheehan said.

"I don't know," she said. "They're green and about a quarter of an inch long. And they bite."

"We haven't seen any, either," Bullard said. "What are you girls ricing for — to sell? Or just for yourselves?"

"Are you kidding?" the ricer said. "We're ricing to sell. It's too expensive to keep."

"Gosh, yes," the other girl said.

"Well," Bullard said. "It looks like you've got about thirty pounds there already."

"Oh, I hope so," the ricer said.

Our boats began to move apart. The other boat was drifting with the breeze. It drifted slowly away, with the girl in the stern using her pole only for steering. Sheehan pushed us off half into the wind, toward the wooded eastern shore. There were splashes there of yellow and orange among the dingy greens. The sugar maples were already turning.

"Nice girls," Bullard said. "But I wish they knew more about ricing. Did you take a look at their rice? It was mostly trash."

"It didn't look like the rice in that other boat," I said.

"No," he said. "But that wasn't any too clean. See if you can't find us a couple of men, Dick — a couple of real ricers."

There were three boats in sight on the eastern side of the lake. The rice grew shorter here, and Sheehan could see the poles and the heads of the polers across the waving field. One of the boats was far to the right of us, working to windward toward the southern arm of the lake. The others were off to the left. We swung left with the breeze and moved up the lake in its steady thrust. The nearer boat was a red canoe. It was working slowly along behind a thin screen of rice at the edge of a patch of open water, and the ricers were both men. We slipped across the open water. There was something familiar about the man with the flails. We came closer, and he turned his head. He was the warden we had seen on the pier.

"How you doing?" Bullard said.

The warden smiled. "We're getting some rice," he said.

"So I see," Bullard said.

So did I. We had come up alongside the boat and were moving with it a few feet off its flank, and I could see their load of rice. The rice came up and over the warden's knees. I also saw something else. I saw what Bullard had meant by trash. This rice was very different from the rice in the other boats. It had a different texture and a different color. It was almost entirely composed of hulls, and most of the hulls were the dead-ripe purple hulls.

Bullard sat looking at the rice. "You must have a good two hundred pounds there," he said.

"We'll get more than that," the warden said.

"It's good-looking, too," Bullard said. "Good and clean."

bilge water, and heaved two bags of rice into the trunk.

Bullard turned and watched them drive away. "Maybe we ought to move on up to the clearing," he said. "The buyers should be there by now. I want to see what they're paying."

We followed the car up the track.

"What do they usually pay?" I said.

"It depends on the size of the crop," Sheehan said. "Last year, the price went up to a dollar sixty-five a pound."

"They won't get that this year," Bullard said.

Another car came down the track. We stepped back into the brush to let it pass, and then went on in its settling dust. Two trucks with spring scales fixed to their tailgates were parked together in the middle of the clearing. The first truck had a hand-lettered paper sign on the door: PATSON — RICE BUYER. Patson was a white man with a gray crew cut and a little black mustache. He was talking to an Indian woman in a long black dress and sneakers.

"No," he said. "I live down in Menahga."

"O.K.," the woman said. "How much you paying?"

"A dollar forty-five," he said. "That's forty-five cents too much, but I don't care about that."

The woman laughed.

"Seriously," he said. "This is a big crop, and the price isn't going to be high. Nobody's going to get rich this year."

The woman laughed again. "I don't get rich last year," she said.

Bullard and Sheehan had walked on to the other truck. They were standing in a group of ricers at the tailgate, and I joined them there. One of the ricers was the man with the tattooed heart. The truck was a big, boxy, slat-sided grain van. There were four bags of rice piled up on the tailgate, and just inside the van was a man sitting on a stool with a ledger in his lap and a metal cashbox at his feet. The buyer was standing with Bullard and Sheehan and the others. He was an Indian — a tall man in rimless glasses and a shiny gray straw fedora.

Bullard introduced me. "Meet Bernard Martin," he said. "Bernie's one of the big buyers around here. He's also chairman of the White Earth Reservation Business Committee."

Martin put out his hand. "Glad to know you," he said.

A voice behind us said, "Hey, Bernie." It was the woman in the black dress and sneakers. "What you paying, Bernie?" she said.

"Oh," Martin said. "Hello, there. Why, we're up to a dollar forty-five today."

"O.K.," the woman said. "I tell him."

A car drove up from the landing as she moved away, and two men got out and unloaded three bags of rice. They dropped them on the ground near the scale. I looked over at Patson. He was standing there all alone.

"You seem to be doing all the business," I said to Martin.

He shrugged. "They know me," he said. "And I try to give them a break. I don't open the sack and look at the rice unless I can feel the sand and gravel and junk like that inside. That doesn't happen too often. I got two rules. I dock them a pound if the sack is wet. If it's so wet the water runs out, then I dock them two or three pounds." He turned to the ricers with the three bags of rice. "Hello, there. We're up to a dollar forty-five today."

The ricers exchanged a glance, and nodded.

"O.K.," Martin said. He picked up one of the bags and hung it by the string around its neck on the hanging hook of the scale. The two ricers stood rigid, watching the indicator sink and leap and settle. "Twenty-three pounds. O.K.?" The ricers nodded. Martin slung the bag on the tailgate and looked up at the man with the ledger. "Twenty-three," he said.

The second bag was heavier. One of the ricers had to help Martin get it on the hook. It weighed fifty-six pounds. The third bag weighed forty-nine pounds. Martin looked at the scale and put a cigarette in his mouth. "Forty-nine pounds," he said. "But what the hell — I'll call it fifty. You guys always get good rice."

"O.K., Bernie," one of the ricers said.

"Fifty," the man with the ledger said. "Twenty-three, fifty-six, and fifty, at a dollar forty-five a pound. That's one hundred and eighty-seven dollars and five cents." He opened the cashbox and counted out the money, and Martin handed it on to one of the ricers.

"Where are you guys ricing tomorrow?" he said.

"Down in the Refuge," the ricer with the money said.

"Well, maybe I'll see you there."

There were many ricers coming up from the landing now, and there were canoes on the roof racks of many of the parked cars. A few of the ricers stopped and spoke to Patson, but all but two or three of them came on to Martin. Most of the ricers had two good-sized bags of rice. I saw the two girls we had met on the lake with a bag of rice that looked as if it might weigh forty pounds, and the woman and the boy, and, leaning against a tree and looking sourly on, the warden from the bridge. The woman and the boy were in a Plymouth station wagon, and the boy was at the wheel. He pulled up at the van, and the woman leaned across him and put her head out the window. "What you paying?" she said. "Dollar forty-five?"

"That's right," Martin said.

The woman shook her head. She sat back and the boy jammed the car into gear, and they drove off through the clearing and out toward the county road.

"She didn't like the price," I said.

"There're quite a few like that," Martin said. "They're always betting on the come. They like to

89

hold out for more money. Sometimes they get it. But this looks like a big crop year, and the price may not go up. It could go down."

"It sure could," Bullard said.

"You think wild rice will be cheaper?" I said.

"You mean at the store?" he said. "I doubt it. There's never that much rice. And it goes through too many different hands. The ricers and the buyers, like Bernie here, are only the beginning. The ricer sells to the buyer and the buyer sells to the processor and the processor sells to the food company — like Uncle Ben or one of those — and the food company sells to the food jobber and the food jobber sells to the store and the store sells to you. That's why the ricer gets a dollar forty-five a pound and you pay ten."

"It's eleven in New York," I said.

We stood and watched the buying. We couldn't leave until the crowd thinned out enough to let us drive down to the landing and pick up our canoe. The last in was the last out. But the afternoon sun was hot, and the cars and the dust and the crowding ricers made it even hotter, and after a while we moved around to the side of the van and sat down in a square of shade. Down on the lake, the wind was blowing hard. It was no longer just a breeze. The rice was whipping and thrashing. It was impossible to tell where the boats had been. It all had a trampled look.

"Bernie must be quite an operator," Sheehan said. "I was talking to his clerk. Do you know how much cash they carry in that box? They drove in here today with twenty thousand dollars."

"They spend it, too," Bullard said. "I don't know if they will today. I only counted about forty boats. But I've seen them pay out that much money in a single afternoon."

A man came around the side of the van. It was the warden. He saw us and smiled and held up a handful of money. "Three hundred and fifty-some bucks," he said. "Not bad for a couple of guys for three hours' work."

"Congratulations," Bullard said.

The warden went smiling on across the clearing.

Bullard cleared his throat. "It *is* good money," he said. "The only trouble is that two or three weeks of ricing is all the real cash that most of these people ever see all year."

South of Ajo

▲▲▲

WE HAD MET for breakfast at the Copper Coffee Shop on the plaza in Ajo, a little copper-mining town in the Sonoran Desert of southern Arizona, and we had drunk the last of our coffee and were ready to go by eight o'clock. As we came out and crossed the covered sidewalk to the car, the trees that shaded the plaza looked dim and dusty in the glare of the bright spring sky, and the air was already warm. The car was nosed up to the curb. It was a pale-green International Scout, and lettered on the hood, in darker green, was PARK RANGER. Two sweating canvas water bags were hung just over the headlights. We took off our jackets and got in and settled down among our gear, and drove off around the plaza. The trees in the plaza were palms and oleanders, and the oleanders were ablaze with hot-pink blossoms.

There were four of us — James Carrico, Richard Cunningham, Max Edwards, and I. Carrico was chief ranger at the Organ Pipe Cactus National Monument, some twenty miles south of Ajo, and Cunningham was chief naturalist there. Organ Pipe Monument is bounded on the east by the Papago Indian Reservation, on the south by Mexico, and on the west by a stretch of mountainous desert known as the Cabeza Prieta Game Range. The game in the Cabeza Prieta Range includes pronghorn antelope, mule deer, peccary, and desert bighorn sheep. Like the Monument, the Game Range is owned and administered by the federal government, but because of past concessions both are vulnerable to exploitation by cattle growers and mining interests, and the Department of the Interior was preparing to propose* to Congress that the two areas be combined to form a preserve called the Sonoran Desert National Park. The Monument comprises around five hundred square miles of land, and the Game Range nearly fourteen hundred. Together, they would make a park almost the size of Delaware. Edwards was Assistant to the Secretary of the Interior and Legislative Counsel of the Department, and he and I had come out to Arizona to spend a couple of days on the Cabeza Prieta trails. Carrico and Cunningham were here to show us around.

We emerged from the plaza. Carrico was at the wheel of the Scout, and I had the seat beside him.

* The proposal has not yet been made.

The others sat on a wooden bench in back. Cunningham had a pair of binoculars around his neck and a
bird guide in his lap. We drove past an adobe Catho-
lic church and an adobe Methodist church and down
a block of crowded houses and across the tracks of
the Tucson, Cornelia & Gila Bend Railroad. Beyond
the tracks was a big, fuming copper-smelting plant,
and beyond the plant the street converged with a
highway that ran between two big piles of green and
gray and red mine tailings. They were enormous piles.
They stood two or three hundred feet high, and they
flanked the highway for two or three miles. Half a
mile beyond the tailings, Carrico turned off the highway and onto a gravel road that led due south.
There were gravelly flats on each side of the road,
and big purple mountains in the distance. The flats
looked as hard and dry and dead as the road, but
scattered here and there were clumps of shiny green
creosote bush gleaming with yellow buttercup flowers. I remembered Mary Austin's apothegm "The
desert begins with the creosote." An adobe house
came into view on the right. The roof had fallen in,
and the dooryard was overgrown with creosote bush.
An overgrown tire track ran up to the house from
the road.

"There's a lonely sight," I said.

"There used to be some Indians living there,"
Carrico said. "I guess their well went dry. That's
what usually happens."

97

"It happens all the time," Cunningham said. "The water table is falling everywhere in this part of the country."

The gravel road came to an end. A bumpy track led on across the creosote desert. The big mountains in the south had come much closer, and there were other, bigger mountains rising now to the east and west, but only the distant mountains now were purple. The nearer mountains had turned a dark rusty red. Cacti began to appear among the creosote bush. Most of the cacti were tall, prickly, tree-trunk saguaro cactus, but there were also a few organ-pipe cactus. The organ-pipe looked a lot like organ pipes. They also looked a lot like thick, upthrusting fingers. The saguaro cactus was variously shaped. Some were merely soaring columns, and some had one or two or three or many raised or twisted or downstretched arms. One had a single pincushion knob growing out of its flank. Many of the saguaros were pierced with woodpecker holes.

Carrico sat up in his seat. "It looks like we're coming out of the flats," he said. "You can always tell by the cactus. The saguaro will rarely grow on the hard-packed desert floor. It likes the slopes, where the soil is a little looser."

"And where it gets a little runoff," Cunningham said.

"Some of those shapes are pretty weird," I said.

"They get that way with age," Carrico said. "I understand they don't even begin to grow any arms until they're forty or fifty years old. But they live to be around two hundred."

"It's probably more than just age," Cunningham said. "There's a theory now that the saguaro's arms are counterweights. The idea is they grow where they're needed for balance. I think that's an interesting explanation. Those saguaros are heavy. They're around ninety per cent water, you know. A big one will weigh several tons. So they have to be kept erect. Because once they start to lean —"

"Watch it," Carrico said.

We jolted down and across and out of a deep wash. The dry bed of the wash was ribbed with sand as fine as beach sand, and along the bank were thickets of salt bush broom and stands of thorny mesquite and paloverde. There were finches moving in the mesquite, and perched on a high branch was a little black phainopepla with a big black crest. The paloverde trees were big enough to cast a carpet of shade, and with their smooth green trunks and smooth green branches and smooth green leaves they looked strangely lush and cool. On the other side of the wash, the track was worse than before. We dropped from fifteen to ten to five miles an hour, and a great cloud of dust rose up and around us. Carrico coughed, and cranked up his window, and after a moment I cranked up mine. Almost at once, my skin prickled with sweat. Carrico took off his sunglasses and wiped them dry and put them on again. We sweltered on through the dust for another mile or two, and then Carrico took his foot off the accelerator. We came to a stop, and the cloud of dust subsided. Carrico pushed open his door.

"Ten o'clock," he said. "Time for a stretch and a drink of water."

I followed him out and around to the front of the car and helped him unfasten one of the canvas water bags. There was a stir of air across the creosote flats, and I could feel my shirt drying on my back, stiffening and pulling away from my skin. Cunningham and Edwards joined us, and we passed the sweating water bag around. The water had a musty, drygoods taste from the canvas, but it was cool, and I held my breath and drank three or four big swallows. I handed the bag to Edwards. He took it and raised it to his mouth, and stopped.

"Listen!" he said. "Just listen! My God, you can't hear a sound. This is a pleasure I haven't had in a long time." He drank and corked the water bag and hung it back on the car. "Where are we, anyway?"

"Well, let's see," Carrico said. "We really aren't anywhere yet. Those are the Ajo Mountains there to the east, and the Growlers off to the northwest. Those up ahead are the Bates Mountains. The mountains behind the Bates are the Puerto Blanco Mountains. If you look beyond that high peak there in the Puerto Blancos, you'll see another peak. It's kind of faint. It's forty miles away. But that's in Mexico."

"Cubabi Peak," Cunningham said.

"That's right," Carrico said. "Cubabi Peak. And this track we're on is called the Bates Well Road. We're headed for Bates Well. It's just inside the Monument. Then we'll cut through a corner of the Monument and into the Game Range. I thought we'd eat lunch at the next well — Papago Well, they call it. Not that we need any water, but it makes a place to stop. There's a certain amount of shade there."

"That sounds great," Edwards said. He got out a pipe and filled it with sweet tobacco and lighted it. "But, my God," he said, "did you ever hear anything so quiet?"

"That's the thing about the desert," Carrico said.

There was a clump of flowering creosote bush at the edge of the track. I picked a blossom and smelled it. It didn't seem to have much smell. The only thing I could smell was Edwards' sweet tobacco.

"Try this," Cunningham said, and broke off a sprig of creosote leaves.

I didn't have to put it to my nose. It had a smell I could smell a foot away — the hot, bitter, smoky smell of creosote. But it had more bite than commercial creosote, and there was something repellent about it. I tossed the sprig away and wiped my hand on my pants. It had a laboratory smell.

"I see what you mean," I said.

"Yes," Cunningham said. "But, of course, it has

101

no connection with the creosote they use to preserve
wood. That's a wood-tar derivative. Creosote bush
is an interesting plant. It's probably the best adapted
of all the desert plants. It will grow in any desert soil
and in almost any aridity. It also has a way of keep-
ing down competition. You notice how those clumps
are ten or fifteen feet apart? That's the spread of
the root system, and it's a kind of free zone. The
roots secrete some toxic substance that keeps most
other plants away, and so the creosote gets whatever
moisture there is. Also, the leaves are coated with
something like a varnish that reduces evaporation.
And that isn't all. The creosote is completely
equipped to survive. It has the kangaroo rat and
other rodents to spread its seeds, and it has no trouble with cattle or sheep. No grazing animal will
touch it. They don't like that creosote smell."

"You know what they say," Carrico said. "Everything in the desert either stinks, stings, or
scratches."

We drove on in another sweltering cloud of dust.
There were many sandy washes now, and the going
got worse and worse. We were coming off the desert
floor. I watched the mountains getting closer and the
smooth sides breaking into rocky cliffs and the color
of the rock brightening in the sun from purple to red
to pink. Landslide foothills tumbled down toward
the track, and there were groves of saguaro cactus
on the slopes. Mingled with the saguaros were clus-

ters of barbed green ocotillo whips and an occasional thrust of organ-pipe cactus. Except for a feathering of opening buds at the tip ends of the whips, the ocotillos looked dry and dead. The only flowers were still the creosote blossoms. Cunningham touched me on the shoulder and pointed, and I caught a glimpse of the zebra back of a Gila woodpecker perched on the side of a raised saguaro arm. The track cut around a little rise. Carrico followed it around — and stepped hard on the brake. Facing us about a dozen feet away were two big staring heifers. They were strange-looking animals. They had the white faces and the red flanks of a Hereford, but their horns were the saber horns of a Texas longhorn. It wasn't only their looks that were strange. They had a quality of strangeness.

"Well," Carrico said. He raced the engine, and the heifers started and stepped back a step or two. But their heads stayed down and their eyes still stared. "They're not feral," he said. "They belong to somebody. They're wild, though. They're wild as hell. It's possible they've never seen a man or a car close up before. I sure wouldn't want to try and pet one of them."

"They probably belong to the Grays," Cunningham said. "That's a family that still has grazing rights in the Monument. And it's like Jim says. They let their cattle range until they're ready to sell them. In this country, you don't have to watch your cattle.

They won't wander off too far. They're tied to your well and watering trough. They've got to come in every two or three days to drink. That's a certain advantage. The disadvantage is that unless you've got a lot of land you can't run many cattle. This dry country wasn't made for cattle. It takes about one square mile to maintain three or four head. Three or four is the maximum."

"In a wet year," Carrico said.

"How much rain is a wet year?" I said.

"Well," he said, and looked at the standing heifers. He raced the engine again, and the heifers stood back a few more steps. That cleared the way. We bumped on down the track. "Nine or ten inches, I guess. Ten inches of rain would make a pretty wet year in this particular area. And this around here is about the best of the desert. It gets drier further west."

"It gets a lot drier," Cunningham said. "The western third of the Game Range gets less than four inches a year. That's real desert. There's nothing more arid than that anywhere in the United States."

"Not even Death Valley?" Edwards said.

"Not even Death Valley," Cunningham said.

Bates Well was a ramshackle ranch. It was deep in the mountains. The track led us up to a barbed-wire fence, and the fence led along to a gate. Just inside the gate was the ranch house. It was a low

white house, with an outer vestibule like a country
church and a corrugated-iron roof, and it sat in the
shade of a tamarisk tree. Beyond the house were a
rickety girder windmill, a water tank on stilts, and a
one-room shack, and farther on, built against a windbreak of mesquite, was a complex of corrals. The
corrals were empty, and the shades in the house were
drawn. Even the windmill was still.

"Civilization," Edwards said.

"We'll take a look," Carrico said.

I got out in the sun and unlatched the gate. Carrico drove through and on to the house. I closed the
gate and cut across a yard of cactus and creosote
bush and patches of thin yellow grass. The others
had the water bag out and open. I joined them. The
house was as closed as it looked.

"Nobody home," Carrico said. "I guess they're
over at one of their other places. They've got a couple of others. But they won't care if we look around
a little. You can see what a difference a little water
makes. Like this grass, for instance, and the size of
those mesquites back there."

"That tamarisk tree is the biggest difference,"
Cunningham said. "They brought that in from somewhere. Tamarisk doesn't grow in the desert."

A path led back to the corrals. I could hear a Gila
woodpecker calling from somewhere out of sight. It
was a quacking, ducklike call. The path led past the
water tank, and an Indian with a big, lined face was

squatting there in the shade, working with a wrench on a pipe fitting. He looked at us without expression. Carrico smiled and nodded.

"Hi there," he said.

The Indian said nothing.

"Chico is bilingual," Carrico said. "But his languages are Papago and Spanish."

"There's a Say's phoebe in that paloverde there," Cunningham said. "A lot of them winter down here."

We walked on to the corrals. Mistletoe was growing in gray cottony clusters in most of the trees in the mesquite windbreak. The corrals were strongly fenced, and equipped with heavy gates. A watering trough, some twenty feet long and four feet wide, was built against one side of the first corral. It was full to the brim with dusty water. A big mesquite overhung the gate, and one long, thin, bending branch was festooned with rusty little cow-pony shoes.

There was a sudden grinding creak behind us. It was the windmill moving in a sudden spring of wind. The vanes creaked into a wild, clattering spin. The wind was a freak of thermal pressures — a dust devil. It shifted away from the windmill and came twisting down the path in a gust of sandy dust. It thrashed in the big mesquite at the gate. It pulled my shirt and tousled my hair. It twisted a column of dust across the front corral, and then came twisting back. It touched the watering trough with a whirl and a splash. Then it twisted across the corral again, and off through the windbreak trees. The air was perfectly still. The windmill had stopped, and I could hear a woodpecker pecking. I looked at Carrico. He was rubbing his eyes. He laughed.

"That's another thing about the desert," he said.

Carrico slowed the car and stopped. We were about a mile beyond Bates Well. He started up again, peering through the windshield, and then turned off the track and onto a just perceptible trace. It was no more than a print of tires in the gravel.

"This is a little detour," he said. "I understand one of the big copper companies has a prospecting crew down here in what they call the Growler Wash, and I'd like to check it out. It won't take long."

We followed the trace through creosote and cactus and tumbled stones. There were mountains close on every side, and the bare pink rock looked fiercely hot in the sun. The trace led into a steep, gullied valley. It was rough riding. We came up over the top of a rise. Just below, at the edge of a wash, were two parked trucks and a big orange core-drilling rig. Carrico pulled up and got out and walked down the slope. Three men in wide straw hats and Wellington boots came out from behind the rig, and one of them came on to meet him. We sat in the Scout and watched them talking. The prospector looked off into space. Then he dug a design in the dust with the toe of his boot. He spat, and Carrico nodded. After a moment, he nodded again, and then turned and came back up to the car. He had a satisfied look on his face.

"Well?" Cunningham said.

"Not too bad," Carrico said, and started the car. He swung it around and we headed back along the trace. "They don't talk much, but I gathered that they're down six hundred feet and they haven't found anything yet."

"So far so good," Cunningham said.

"Yes," Carrico said. He turned to me. "It's an awkward situation. What these people are doing is perfectly legal, you know. They have a perfectly legal claim and every right to work it. But that doesn't mean that it's good. We think it's wrong. We think it's the most adverse use of this kind of land you can find. It's exactly what the proposed Sonoran Desert National Park is intended to prevent."

"It *is* wrong," Cunningham said. "This is unspoiled, pristine desert. There's nothing quite like it anywhere else in the country. But suppose they find copper back there. You saw those mountains of tailings up in Ajo. That would be one result. The other would be a monstrous open-pit mine. The one in Ajo is a crater that covers almost five hundred acres and is almost eight hundred feet deep. This desert is fragile. A scar like that would last till the end of time."

"And erosion would make it worse," Carrico

said. "But even if they don't make a find, they'll
leave a mess. They always do."

It was after one o'clock when we drove into Papago Well. The place had a long-abandoned look.
There were two roofless shacks and a five-foot con-
crete water-storage tank on one side of the track and
the remains of a stone foundation and a padlocked
shed on the other. A paloverde tree grew near the
door of the shed, and behind the shed, in a tumbledown log corral, was a cement watering trough
about the size of a bathtub. The trough held water. I
could see the shine of it in the sun. But Papago Well
was nothing like Bates Well. The paloverde was the
only tree much bigger than a bush. There was still
the feel of the desert.

"What happened here?" Edwards said. "It
looks like a ghost town."

"I doubt if it ever was much of a town," Carrico
said. "But I don't know its history. It's been like this
for a good many years. About all it is now is a water
hole for wildlife. The Bureau of Sport Fisheries and
Wildlife has a man that comes around and keeps the
pump and everything in order. This is the only water
in this part of the Game Range." He nosed the car in
under the big paloverde. A bevy of six or seven Gam-
bel's quail burst across the corral, running hard with
black plumes waving, and then hopped into the air
and sailed off into the creosote. We climbed out and

stretched and had a drink of water from the water bag. It felt good to be out of the car and in the open air. Our lunch was packed in two cardboard boxes, and Cunningham carried them across the track to an edge of shade in front of the storage tank. We sat there comfortably out of the sun and drank tomato juice and ate hard-boiled eggs and liverwurst sandwiches and raw carrots. The carrots were crisp and cool and delicious in the heat. We finished lunch with raisin cake and coffee from a Thermos. Edwards lighted up his perfumed pipe. I lay back against the wall of the tank and listened to the quail chirping and calling somewhere off across the track. The sky overhead was an empty, faded blue. It was completely empty — no planes, no vapor trails, no clouds of any kind. Carrico poured himself a second cup of coffee.

"You know," he said, "I often think about the old-timers who crossed this desert in the old days. It's rough enough in a Scout or a Jeep. But those guys did it on horseback or in wagons or on foot. You wonder how they managed about water. There is only one permanent spring in the whole Game Range, and the spring at Quito Baquito is the only reliable spring in the Monument."

"I guess a lot of them didn't manage," Cunningham said. "That's why the trail they used was called the Camino del Diablo."

"The Devil's Highway," Edwards said.

"Yes," Carrico said. "As a matter of fact, you can still get in trouble here. If your car breaks down or you run out of gas or something, you had better know what to do. Especially in the summer. We get temperatures here as high as a hundred and eighty degrees at ground level, and a temperature like that can dehydrate a man pretty fast. I know one recent instance. There was a young ranger at the Monument had his car break down in this desert. It was a day in July, but he was only about twelve miles from headquarters, so he decided to walk. He made it — but just barely. He was really sweated out. He collapsed and had to be helped in, and he lay in the bathtub soaking up water for about four hours before he began to feel alive again. And it took him a couple of days to get all the way back to normal. An experienced man would never have taken a chance like that. He would at least have waited till sundown."

"Or just waited for help to come," Cunningham said. "I wouldn't want to walk across this desert on a summer night. Night is when the rattlesnakes come out. That's their time to hunt. They can't stand the daytime heat."

"Dick's right," Carrico said. "It's probably best to just sit tight and wait. Nobody goes out in the desert without telling somebody where he plans to go. When one of us goes out, we always file a route. I had to file one this morning."

"Where are we going from here?" I said.

"I thought we'd go down to the border," he said. "Down into what they call the O'Neill Hills. Then I thought we'd head toward the Agua Dulce Mountains and spend the night somewhere up around Papago Mountain. That's good, rough country, but we've got plenty of water, so we can camp anywhere we like. And in the morning I thought we'd go back by way of Quito Baquito. That's the spring I mentioned a minute ago. Actually, it's a pond, and a pretty one. We ought to get there around noon. They expect us back at headquarters by midafternoon. If we don't show up by around that time, they'll send somebody out to find us."

Cunningham sat up. "Look!" he said. "Off there to the —" He sat back. "Never mind. It's just a redtail. For a moment, it looked like an eagle."

A few hundred yards from Papago Well, the track broke into a fork. One fork led northwest and the other led west. A signpost stood between them, and the sign on the northwest fork read, MOHAWK 52 M. NO PERMANENT WATER ON THIS ROAD. The other sign read, TULE WELL 31 M. TINAJAS ALTAS 50 M. Below that was an arrow pointing back the way we had come and marked. BATES WELL 23 M. We took the Tule Well fork.

It was a much better track than the one before. It soon became almost a road. Carrico shifted into high for the first time since midmorning, and we moved along at a good fifteen miles an hour. There was less dust now, and we opened the windows and the blowing air was warm but not unpleasant. The desert also began to change. There were new green leaves on the ocotillo whips along the track, and here and there among the creosote were patches of new grass and even patches of flowers — yellow desert marigold, pink and lavender globe mallows, creeping purple-mat, little desert sunflowers. The sunflowers and the globe mallows were swarming with tiny white moths.

"There must have been some rain along here," I said.

"There must have been quite a bit," Cunningham said. "Most of those flowers are annuals, and it takes a good rain to bring them up. The seeds they drop will sometimes lie dormant for years. They will germinate only after a couple of good, hard rains. That's an interesting phenomenon, and it used to be a big botanical mystery. But the explanation is simply this: The seeds of the desert annuals are covered with a water-resistant skin that will only dissolve in a rain that brings enough moisture to assure the growth of the plant. How's that for survival technique? If a shower was enough to germinate the seed, the species would never survive."

The rain had been a very local rain. After a couple of miles, the grass and the flowers began to peter out, and after another mile they were gone. We were back in the empty creosote flats. They seemed emptier than ever. I gazed across the flats at the mountains on the horizon up ahead. One of the peaks was strangely shaped and colored. It looked like a big dark brick mounted on a mound of bright white marble. I borrowed Cunningham's binoculars. The brick was brown volcanic rock and the base it stood on was granite, but it still looked like a brick.

"That's where the Game Range gets its name," Carrico said. "Those mountains are the Cabeza Prieta Mountains, and that biggest peak is Cabeza Prieta Peak. The old Spaniards gave it that name way back in the seventeenth century."

"Cabeza Prieta," Edwards said. "Oh, I get it — Dark Head."

"That's right," Carrico said. "Cabeza Prieta is one of the few good landmarks around here. And it's fairly high for the Sonoran Desert. It must be at least twenty-five hundred feet."

"It doesn't look that high," I said.

"Well," he said, "it's about thirty miles away."

That was about as close as we got to the Cabeza Prieta Mountains. The track soon took a new direction, swinging away from west to south, and first the lesser peaks and then Cabeza Prieta itself sank out of sight. We passed under the loom of a rocky hill and into a narrow valley. There were many fallen rocks on the valley floor, and the flanking slopes were grown with organ-pipe cactus and saguaro cactus and prickly-pear and barrel cactus and chain-fruit cholla cactus. Edwards leaned forward.

"Hey," he said. He pointed to a rectangular pile of stones near the track with a rusty iron cross stuck up at one end. "That looks like a grave over there."

"It is a grave," Carrico said. "It's the grave of

an old prospector named David O'Neill. He's the man they named these hills for."

"He drowned," Cunningham said.

Edwards laughed.

"No kidding," Cunningham said. "He died of drowning."

"They found him face down in a wash," Carrico said. "I guess he got caught in a flash flood."

"That happens every now and then," Cunningham said. "The desert is a very strange place."

We came to the end of the valley. Beyond the flanking hills were creosote flats that stretched far away south to a sudden rise of sawtooth mountains. The track skirted the edge of the flats and then cut sharply off to the right, heading west again. Carrico stopped the car.

"This is as far south as we go," he said. "We can't go any further. That's Mexico straight ahead. The border runs through those flats." He sat back and stretched. "If you'd like to really see it, we could climb that hill. There's a real great view from up there."

"All right," I said.

"Let's go," Edwards said. "I'd be glad to stretch my legs. How about you, Dick?"

"I think I'll just stay here," Cunningham said. "I've climbed that hill. It's higher than it looks. It's close to six hundred feet."

"That's why it's such a great view," Carrico said.

We went up the slope to the foot of the hill.

From there, it looked like more than a hill. It was
the same pink granite as the mountains, and it rose
up from the slope at a mountainous pitch. It was almost as steep as a stepladder. Carrico led the way up
the easiest face. We went on all fours, but it wasn't
difficult climbing. There were plenty of toehold
ledges and outcrops. A few feet from the top, I
looked back. Edwards was just below me, and just
below him was a bulge of rock. Below that was nothing but space on down to the valley floor and the little green lump of the car. If Cunningham was right
about the height of the hill, I was looking down from
the top of a forty-story building. It was a moment
before I had the strength to go on.

The top of the hill was a narrow ridge. It was
broken into several levels, and Carrico was waiting
for us on the highest, with his hair blowing wild in
the wind. The rock of the hilltop was hot to the
touch. I stood carefully up well back from the edge
— and Carrico was right. There was a great view. I
wasn't ready to look down again, but I didn't mind
looking into the distance. Edwards came scrambling
up beside me. We stood there getting our breath and
looked out at the spread of the desert — at an im-
mensity of flats and hills and range after range of
mountains climbing around the horizon. It was a
really great view, but I couldn't really enjoy it. All I
could think about was the climb back down.

We went down a different face. The first two
hundred feet were the steepest and hardest, and they

took us almost as long as the whole of the upward climb. Then came a tier of shelflike ledges. And then the worst was over. Below the shelves was a long, easy gravel slide. We went sloshing down through the gravel. Edwards let out a whooping laugh.

"If I fall off this hill," he said, "I have one last request. I want to be buried up next to O'Neill."

I was laughing, too. It was only a few more yards to the bottom. "All right," I said. "And we'll change the name of these hills to the Edwards-O'Neill Hills."

"I'd appreciate that," he said. "But you know, of course, what will happen. People will begin to drop the 's' in Edwards and forget the hyphen, and pretty soon it will be the Edward O'Neill Hills."

"That's a problem," I said.

"It's hopeless," Carrico said.

We drove back up the valley. The drive down the valley seemed a long time ago. We passed O'Neill's grave and headed back across the creosote flats, and Cabeza Prieta raised its head again in the west. It was after four when we turned off the track and onto a rutted trail that led eastward toward the Agua Dulce Mountains. We dropped down to ten and then to five miles an hour. The trail crossed and recrossed a winding wash, and then turned and followed its southern bank. A big, humped, sunbaked mountain rose abruptly up from the desert ahead. That would be Papago Mountain. It was three or four times the height of the O'Neill hill we had climbed, and as we came under its loom it blocked the eastern sky.

We made camp in a grassy bend of the wash. It was sheltered on the south by a steep embankment and on the north and west by trees — mesquite, paloverde, and tesota ironwood. The ironwoods were the first I had seen. They were dense, black-barked trees with bluish, fernlike evergreen leaves. Cunningham, Edwards, and I unloaded the car and set up our cots and sleeping bags under the protective lip of the embankment. There was no need for a tent. It wasn't going to rain. By the time we had finished, Carrico had gathered an armload of ironwood twigs and sticks and got a cooking fire going. The ironwood smoke had a faintly cinnamon smell. I stood by the fire for a moment, feeling the satisfaction of a comfortable camp, and then walked up the wash through a panic of scattering lizards to get more wood. Tesota ironwood is among the hardest of North American woods, and it makes fine coals for cooking. There was plenty of it to be had. Dead branches hung from most of the ironwood trees. But five or six branches the size of my wrist were about all I could carry at a time. They had the weight of iron pipe. Cunningham joined me on my second trip, and Edwards got an axe and broke up the wood we brought in. The ironwood was actually too hard to cut. It could only be hacked and splintered.

When the wood was in, the camp was made. We settled down at the fire, and Edwards found some paper cups and passed around a bottle of Scotch and the water bag. The fire felt as good as the whiskey. Papago Mountain was still bright with sunlight, but the light was the blaze of sunset, and the heat was going out of the day. I looked at my watch. It was twenty minutes past six. Carrico put a grill over the fire and sliced some little pink new potatoes into a frying pan, and then unwrapped four thick strip steaks and arranged them on the grill. Dinner was on the way. He sat back on his heels and held out his cup for another dollop of Scotch. The sunlight on Papago Mountain brightened and flamed as red as the fire. The shade in the wash began to deepen into twilight. Then a shadow appeared at the foot of the mountain. It moved darkly up the mountain face, and suddenly the last of the light was gone. It was suddenly night and suddenly almost cold. A thin new moon rose over the mountaintop.

Carrico served up our steaks and fried potatoes, and put on a pot of coffee. We ate sitting close to the fire, glad of its warmth and light and comfort, and watched the high black sky fill up with stars. The steaks were faintly flavored with the cinnamon ironwood smoke. Far out in the night, a coyote gave a doglike bark and then a banshee wail. Carrico poured the coffee and built up the fire and lighted a long cigar.

"This is my time of day," he said. "There's nothing like it. Not even breakfast."

"This is what it's all about," Edwards said.

I woke up once in the night. The moon had set and the wind was blowing. I looked up at the stars and listened to the wind moving in the trees. It felt strange to be lying there in the desert night, but it also felt very good. The sky was clear and the air was fresh and my sleeping bag was warm. It was even stranger to think of the daytime desert. I turned over on my side and went happily back to sleep.

Fast Water

▲▲▲

WE LEFT THE ranch — the Circle S, a horse-and-cattle ranch that also takes in guests, some thirty miles north of Pinedale (pop. 965), in the Wind River Mountains of western Wyoming — after an early breakfast, and headed up a long, empty gravel road that led to Bridger National Forest. There were three of us and a cowhand driver in an old International Scout, and behind us we towed a big, flat-bottomed rowboat on a trailer. My companions were William A. Worf, the supervisor of Bridger National Forest, and Thomas Scholebo, the foreman of the Circle S and a professional guide and boatman. They sat in the back of the Scout, hunched under the flapping canvas top, holding their big hats on their laps. Scholebo's face was deeply tanned to a point just above the eyebrows, but the skin on his forehead was white. With them was our gear — an insulated lunch bag, a quart Thermos bottle, a couple of jackets, and a pair of hip-length waders. I sat up front with the driver. The road was flanked by sagebrush flats, and there were bluebells and bright-red Indian paintbrush and yellow bitter brush in flower, among the gray-green bushes. Beyond the sagebrush flats rose scattered groves of quaking aspen, and beyond the aspen were forests of lodgepole pine and Engelmann spruce climbing steeply to high green mountain meadows, and above the meadows were granite peaks capped and crevassed with snow. Down on the road, it was hot and dry, and we drove in a haze of yellow dust. We drove for half an hour. Then the road turned right, and we climbed up through the aspens. The aspens gave way to pines, and the road became a track. We emerged from the pines at the foot of a little mountain lake near the head of a mountain river. The lake was Lower Green River Lake, and the river was the Green River and our destination. The Green River, the principal tributary of the Colorado, which it joins in southeastern Utah, was one of several remote and unspoiled rivers that had been proposed* by the Departments of the Interior and Agriculture for inclusion (wholly or in part) in a National Wild Rivers System.† An eighty-four-mile stretch of the Green — from its headwaters in a torrent of springs and glacial creeks just above Upper Green River Lake to a crossroads village just west of Pinedale called Dan-

---

* In 1965.   † The Green River has not yet been included in the system.

iel — had been designated for preservation under this program, and I was there to see what I could of it.

The driver swung the Scout around and backed the trailer down to the edge of the lake. The lake was a brilliant blue in the July sun, but it also looked cold and deep. We all got out, and Worf and Scholebo put their big hats on. We unhitched the boat and hauled it across a pebbly beach and into the water. It was a solid, rough-water boat — a fourteen-foot Mackenzie River boat, with a Fiberglas bottom, a high gunwale, and a high, pointed bow decked over for a couple of feet. Scholebo pulled off his boots and got into the rubber waders. Worf and I stowed the lunch and the jackets away in the cubby under the bow, and Scholebo tossed his boots in after them. Then he waded out and brought the boat about and nodded to us to get aboard. We stepped in and sat down together on a thwart at the bow. Scholebo gave the boat a shove and climbed over the gunwale and took the center thwart. We drifted heavily off. The driver leaned against the door of the Scout and watched us from under the brim of his hat. Scholebo got out a pair of oars and fitted them into oarlocks. He pulled the boat into line. Then he rowed us along the shore of the lake and around a wooded point of land and into the grip of the river.

We moved with the current down a pillared aisle of pines. Scholebo rested on his oars. There was nothing for him to do but keep the boat head on. The water was brown but very clear, and I could see the cobblestone bottom sliding away beneath us. It looked about five feet deep. The pines thinned out and moved back from the river, and willow scrub sprang up along the banks. Beyond the willows were sagebrush flats like those that flanked the road. The road was somewhere off to the left and out of sight behind the sweep of a long wooded ridge. On the right, beyond the flats and the aspen groves and the forests of spruce and pine, the snowy mountains loomed again. At the edge of one of the aspen groves stood a browsing antelope. It raised its head and looked in our direction, and five or six more antelope rose up from the brush. They gazed at us for a moment. Then they turned with a flash of white rumps and trotted up the slope and in among the trees.

"We call them pronghorns," Worf said. "I understand that thirty or forty years ago they were practically extinct, but they've come back very strong. You're apt to see them almost anywhere in this valley — even grazing right along with the cattle." He turned to Scholebo. "The river looks high. I've very seldom seen it as high as this."

"It's real high," Scholebo said. "I think we might have some excitement when we hit fast water today."

"Is there much fast water along here?" I asked.

"I don't know this part of the river too well," Scholebo said. "But I think there's two or three pretty fast stretches. We're coming down from pretty high country, you know. The elevation back there at the lake is over eight thousand feet. We'll run about twenty-five miles — I thought we'd take out at a landing just above the Circle S. We'll have dropped at least three hundred feet by then. Our elevation at the ranch is seventy-eight hundred. That's an average fall of a good twelve feet a mile."

"I know one stretch where the river drops something like sixty feet in only a couple of miles," Worf said.

"You mean just below Roaring Fork Creek?"

"That's right."

"So do I," Scholebo said.

The river widened a little, and the current began to slacken. A slough appeared on the right. Scholebo took up his oars again. Here and there along the riverbanks were the remains of beaver houses. They looked like piles of brush cast up by a flood. A change came over the water. It was still clear. I could still see the cobbly bottom. But the color had changed from brown to a bright and shining green.

"I can see why they call this the Green River," I said.

"It's green, all right," Worf said. "But I don't know. You hear a lot of stories. Some people think like you do. They say the river got its name from the color of the water. Other people say it got its name from the way it keeps this valley green. But the story most people tell is that it got its name from the famous fur trader General Ashley. They say he named it for a friend of his back in St. Louis named Green."

The river wound down through the flower-spangled sagebrush flats. I could smell the dry, peppery, haylike smell of the sage on every breath of breeze. From somewhere out on the flats a meadow lark called its gulping call. The only other sounds were the lap of water against the boat and the creak and rattle of the oars. Worf touched my arm, and pointed to a dark speck high in the sky overhead.

"Hawk?" I asked.

"Golden eagle," he said.

The river crawled around a bend and into a tumble of boulders. They were great, round, hummocky boulders. Some of them were as big as the boat. Most of them were overgrown with a flaming-orange lichen. The lichen burned against the bright-green water with an almost tropical intensity. We moved in among the boulders, and I heard the sound of running water. The sound grew louder. I looked over my shoulder at Scholebo. He smiled.

"Sounds kind of interesting, don't it?" he said.

I felt the current quicken. There was a sudden flash of white up ahead. It was water breaking and boiling over a sunken boulder. Near it was another burst of white water, and, beyond that, still another. I glanced at Scholebo again. He was pushing hard on the oars, pushing against the current, braking the boat against its strengthening pull. His smile was fixed on his face. Then we were in the rapids. The boat gave a skittering lurch. We dropped between two dripping boulders and slewed across a third.

Scholebo wrenched the boat around. We heeled clear of an explosion of spume. The stern went down, and the bow rose up and shuddered and fell away. We tilted down a heaving chute, ground over a seething shoal, and emerged into open water. I looked back up the rapids. They didn't look much longer than forty or fifty yards, but we had dropped six feet or more.

"That was nice work, Tom," Worf said.

"Very nice," I said. "I don't see how you ever followed that channel."

Scholebo's smile relaxed. "Channel?" he said. "There isn't too much channel to follow in water like that. About all you can do is try to stay out of the white stuff."

The river resumed its comfortable course. We moved gently along in a gentle current. The willow banks slipped past at an easy walking pace. A dozen big white ducks sprang up from under the brushy bank on the right. They were mergansers. They ran splashing across the water and out of sight behind a willow island. Up on the flats beyond the island stood a weathered raw-plank shed. It was the first building I'd seen since we left the ranch, and it had a forlorn and lonely look.

"That's a state feed barn," Worf said. "They store hay there for the elk in winter. We've got a herd of four or five hundred head of elk up here, and they can't always make it through to spring without a little help. This is big snow country, you know."

"We get a lot of snow," Scholebo said. "One winter back in the old railroading days, the Union Pacific sent a gang of tie-hackers in here. They cut pine for crossties until spring, and then floated the logs down the river and cleared out. That was a long time ago, but you can still tell where they worked. You can still see the stumps — hundreds of acres of six-foot stumps. That's how deep the snow was that winter. And that was nothing unusual. I've seen twelve foot of snow on the ground at the ranch."

Something moved across the front of the barn. It looked like a big tan dog. It disappeared into the brush.

"Coyote," Worf said.

A rocky ridge far off to the right moved closer to the river, and here and there, thrusting up through the sagebrush on the flats at its foot, were great fists and fingers of granite. Plunging down from the ridge and across the flats was a creek. I could see it foaming among the rocks, and I could hear its surflike rumble. It plunged over a granite shelf and into the river in a thunderclap of spray. Worf sat up in his seat.

"Roaring Fork Creek," he said. "The Green looks a lot like that back up in the mountains where it gets its start. It's just as wild and just as milky. And this is where we hit some real fast water." He turned to Scholebo. "Look at the size of Roaring Fork, Tom. This next fast water is going to be fast."

Scholebo smiled and nodded.

We moved past the mouth of the creek in a sudden surge of current. The roar of Roaring Fork diminished and died away, but up ahead I could hear another, deeper roar. Boulders appeared in the stream bed, and the river suddenly narrowed. The current gave another sudden surge. We swung around a violent wishbone bend and under the flank of an aspen grove and into a torrent of whipping, whitecapped water. It swept us down and across the river. We bumped and scraped and lurched along the face of a wave-swept boulder. Scholebo pulled us off and safely about. We bobbed for a moment in a kind of eddy. Then the current caught us again. We slipped into a deep-green channel between the bank and a boiling boulder shoal. Another fury of white-capped water exploded just ahead. We heeled away to the right — and the bottom fell out of the river. We dropped emptily down an avalanche of froth and foam. The stern rose up, and the bow went deeply down. Worf let out a warning yell. I made a grab for the gunwale. A wall of water broke over the bow and collapsed on Worf and me. It was icily, numbingly cold, and it filled the boat to the thwarts. Another wave broke over the side. We thumped like a log down a hundred feet of chute, and then Scholebo hauled us clear and into a pocket of easier water. We hung there, pitching and sloshing.

"That wasn't so good," he said.

"No harm done," Worf said. "I wasn't wearing my Sunday suit."

Scholebo smiled his absent smile. He leaned hard on the oars, holding the boat in the slack water, and gazed down the river. It looked as bad below us as it did back up above. It looked worse. It was boulders and spray and thrashing water as far as I could see.

"Well," he said. "We'll never make it down the rest of the way like this. This boat is pretty close to swamped." He shifted his grip on the oars. "I guess the only thing is to try to get to shore and empty her out."

The only shore was the willow bank on the left. The other bank was too steep and stony for landing. And the only way was down. We moved across the slack water and wallowed down a shallow riffle. The bottom bumped and scraped on every sunken stone. At the foot of the riffle, the current cut sharply in among the overhanging willows. Scholebo pulled hard to the left, and the boat swung in toward the bank. He shipped the oars and caught up a line and jumped out into water halfway up his thighs. He took a step and slipped. The line went slack, and the boat began to slide downstream. I grabbed a trailing willow branch. The boat gave a lurch and tilted. I went over the side.

When I came up, Worf reached out and got my arm and helped me back into the boat. I came in over the bow. The boat had yawed around in the current and was slopping along the bank stern first. Scholebo was already back aboard. He had the oars, but the willows were in the way and he couldn't get them into the water. A twist of current drew us away from the bank, and Scholebo freed the oars. He brought the boat properly about. We skirted the lip of a chute and lumbered into an eddy and back in among the willows. It was slack water there, and the boat sat as dead as a hulk. Scholebo waded ashore with the line. Worf and I followed him, and the three of us dragged the dead weight of the boat a few feet up through the willows, and unloaded the lunch and the oars and our sodden jackets, and heaved it over on its side. We held it there while the water dumped and poured and dribbled out, and looked at the bottom. The Fiberglas glaze was cobwebbed with tiny scratches and one little thumbnail gash. That would have been the boulder at the very head of the rapids.

Worf looked at his watch. "Five to twelve," he said. "What do you fellows think about lunch? I'm kind of hungry."

"Suits me," Scholebo said. "As a matter of fact, it's either eat now or wait about an hour. These rapids go on for another two or three miles."

I said I was ready, and we gathered up the lunch and the jackets and pushed on through the willows. We came out into a sunny meadow of sage and blooming flowers. The most abundant flower was Indian paintbrush, and it grew in clusters among the sage in several different colors. Most of the blooms were red, but there were also clusters of orange and yellow, and even a delicate apricot pink. Against the background of silvery sage they were very beautiful.

There was no shade in the meadow, but after the waterlogged boat and my fall in the river the hot mountain sun felt good. We took off our shirts and spread them and our jackets on the springy sage to dry. Almost at once, a cloud of little black mosquitoes sprang up around us. They were very small, not much bigger than gnats, but there were thousands of them and they filled the air with a distant, menacing moan. I began to slap at my arms and chest. Scholebo brought out a bottle of insect repellent. He poured some in his palm and handed the bottle to me, and I spread a protective film and passed the bottle on to Worf. The stuff had a pleasant, spicy smell, but the mosquitoes were immediately repelled. They rose to a point an inch or two above our heads and hung there in a seething, heaving, moaning swarm. We squatted comfortably down in a clearing in the sage, and Scholebo opened up the lunch. The mosquitoes followed us down.

"It's funny about these mosquitoes," Scholebo said. "The old stockmen that settled this country didn't feel the way we do about them. They used to say they were glad to see a good crop of mosquitoes. They said mosquitoes meant moisture in the ground, and moisture in the ground meant good hay, and good hay meant fat beef. I think they had a point."

"Worse things can happen to a river than mosquitoes," Worf said.

"You've got a point there, too," Scholebo said, and handed us each a paper bag.

My bag contained a little six-ounce can of Coors Rocky Mountain beer, a thick roast-beef sandwich, an orange, a Hershey bar, a beer-can opener, and an enamelware mug. The others had the same. I opened my beer and unwrapped my sandwich, and Scholebo filled our mugs with coffee from the Thermos. The beer was cold, and at that altitude it had almost the impact of whiskey. I drank it and ate my sandwich and peeled and ate my orange. I left the candy bar in the bag for later. Then I lay back with my coffee and gazed peacefully up at the mountains and the gleam of snow on the peaks and the pale-blue sky beyond. The only thing that kept me awake was the hovering moan of the mosquitoes.

When we got up to go, our clothes were practically dry. My shirt was crisp and warm from the sun, and faintly scented with sage. We packed the remains of our lunch back in the insulated bag and walked down the meadow to the boat. The mosquitoes followed us down the meadow, but most of them peeled away at the edge of the willows, and by the time we had the boat in the water, the last of them were gone. Scholebo shoved off and splashed in over the side and swung the bow around. I felt the current touch it, and we began to move. We moved into smooth but heaving water, in and out of the wrench of a whirlpool, and into the chute we had skirted almost an hour before. It was long and steep and very

fast, but the openings were wide enough for Scholebo to use his oars for braking, and we went down in
grinding rushes and teetering halts and sudden, surg-
ing slides. Below the chute, the openings between the
boulders shrank, and the river began to twist and
turn. We bumped and plunged from boulder to boulder for about a mile. Then the river gradually widened. The current slackened, the chop subsided, the
boulders dwindled away. A scatter of grassy islands
appeared, and we drifted in among them. Like the
sagebrush flats, they were bright with many kinds of
flowers. Worf reached out and picked a handful of
bluebells.

"Down south — down in Utah, in the Wasatch
country — they have whole fields of these," he said.
"Acres and acres of bluebells. They're the primary
sheep feed there. But you never saw anything more
beautiful in your life."

"I've seen them," Scholebo said. "And they're
pretty, all right. But I'll tell you what I like. It's this
green all along this valley, these four different greens
— the willow along the shore, the sage on the flats,
then the quakers on the slopes, and the pines up there
on the crests. That's what I call pretty."

We emerged from the islands. The river was
even wider now, and the high stony bank on the right
had vanished. In its place stretched a marshy wilderness of willow scrub and backwater ponds.

"That looks like moose habitat," Worf said.

"It is," Scholebo said. "And if you want to see a moose, there's a yearling laying down there in the willows." He leaned forward and pointed. "He's just this side of that slough."

I followed his finger and stared. It was an extraordinary sight — a long, brown horsy head, an enormous head, with two enormous, mulelike ears and an expression as sad as a hound's. It watched us drifting closer and closer. Then it unfolded its legs and stood up. It stood as tall as any horse. It turned into the slough and splashed away.

We drifted on in an easy current. Two yellow warblers dodged out of the willows and in again. In the distance, half a mile downstream, a string of six or seven ducks went swinging across the marsh. There was another sound of splashing, and another big head poked through the willows. It was almost immediately joined by another. The two moose watched us for a moment, and then they were gone.

"Another couple of yearlings," Scholebo said.

"Hey," Worf said, pointing off to the right. "There's a cow and her calf."

Two moose were swimming across the end of a pond. Only their heads were showing, one twice the size of the other. Scholebo gave the oars a vigorous pull to the left.

"I guess we're far enough away for comfort," he said. "But I don't want to take any chances. You want to stay away from a pair like that. If a cow

137

moose thinks you're interested in her calf, you can have a real fight on your hands. She'll take anything and anybody on."

"Don't I know it!" Worf said. "She'll climb right into the boat with you. I remember one time I was riding up in the Forest, way back in the Wilderness Area, and I happened to get between a cow moose and her calf. She practically climbed right into the saddle with me. She hit that horse like a ton of bricks. I tell you, we really took off."

The moose came out of the water. The cow was even bigger than the first of the yearlings, and her color was the same dark brown, but the calf was as red as a Hereford. It stopped and raised its head and bawled. It didn't sound much like a frightened calf. The sound was a wild, ferocious blat. The cow turned and looked carefully all around. Then she gave the calf a nudge, and they clambered up the bank and into the willows.

The current petered out, and the boat began to wander. Scholebo took up the oars again. A big black-and-white bird with a long greenish tail hopped out on a willow branch and gave a frantic cry. It was a magpie. It cried again, more frantically than before.

"There's another nervous mother," Scholebo said. "She's got some young ones not too far away."

We floated down along the marsh for a mile or more. There was an almost constant sound of splashing from deep in the sloughs, and once I heard the distant blat of a calf. Then the marshy bank began to rise. The ponds shrank and dried into sloughs, and the sloughs climbed up into sagebrush flats. Scholebo rested on his oars. The current was back again.

"Well, that's the end of the moose for now," Worf said. "We're out of moose habitat. They only like the willow sloughs. But we saw some moose, didn't we? A cow and a calf and three yearlings. I say that's quite a sight. And it isn't one that you can see just anywhere."

"You've got a point there, Bill," Scholebo said. "This is still pretty nice country around here. It's like Bill says — where else can you find what we've got? I've never heard of better trout fishing anywhere than in this river and the creeks that feed it, and we've got moose and elk and deer and prong-horn antelope and bighorn sheep and bear and mountain lion. We've still got every kind of wild life here we ever had — except buffalo. A couple of years ago, I walked into three mountain lions in a bunch. It was up in that high country there — up around Pass Creek. There were two of them laying down, and the other was standing up. They say they won't bother a man, but I got away from there real fast. All I really remember is their tails. They had the longest tails you ever saw. They looked about four feet long."

"What about bear?" I asked.

"Well," he said. "You know that bearskin on the wall to the right of the door at the ranch lodge? The boss's wife got that bear the spring before last up Jim Creek. That's only a couple of miles from the Circle S."

"How about that bearskin on the other wall?" Worf said.

Scholebo laughed. "Oh," he said. "I guess I got that one myself. I got it last fall. Me and another fellow were out after elk. We come up a draw and stopped to rest our horses, and I happened to look up. There was a black bear watching us over a hump in the ridge. I got off my horse and got my rifle and put in a shell, and the bear took off. She took off up the ridge, and just before she reached the top I got my shot. She dropped and began to roll. She rolled down the ridge right for me. I had to jump out of the way or be run over. I climbed up to the hump where I'd seen her and looked around a little and finally found a cave. She'd been cleaning it out and fixing it up for winter. She was a fair-sized bear for a black bear. She dressed out at a little over three hundred pounds."

A little creek tinkled in from the left. The river slowed and widened, and willows began to gather again on the banks. High overhead, a big black bird circled into view. Two smaller birds were darting around it like swallows flighting at dusk. The big bird looked very much like a crow — but a giant crow. It looked as big as the biggest hawk. I turned to follow its flight, and Scholebo looked up from his oars.

"That's a raven," he said. "And those are rusty blackbirds chasing him. Those little birds will go after a raven every chance they get."

"Or a hawk," Worf said.

"That's right," Scholebo said. "They'll take on just about anything. But I guess they're not much more than a nuisance. A raven or a hawk can shake them off any time they like. All he has to do is climb. That's what this fellow is doing right now. He's going way up where the little birds can't follow."

We watched the raven until it was only a speck in the sky. The rusty blackbirds fell slowly back to easier altitudes. Off in the willows I heard a splash, and then an irritable blat. We were back in moose country. It was duck country, too. At every bend, we put up little flocks of mallards or mergansers. Scholebo touched my shoulder, and pointed. It was also goose country. Close to shore, near the mouth of a dribbling creek, sat a Canada goose and a file of four big, fat goslings. The goose let out a warning honk, and the goslings gathered instantly together. She honked again and swung away downstream with the goslings paddling along behind. Big as they were, and they were at least the size of mallards, they were still too young to fly. We trailed them down the river to the mouth of another creek. They slipped in there and disappeared behind a curtain of willows.

"Well, by golly!" Worf said. "I call that another sight worth seeing." He gave a kind of grunt. "You know, there's something about a river. It isn't like a lake or the ocean. I mean, it's always changing. Especially a river like this. You never know what's going to happen next. You never know what you're going to see. Every bend is something new and different."

"It's a pretty good way to spend a day," Scholebo said.

There was a sound of running water off to the right. I looked around at Scholebo.

"That sounds like some more fast water," I said.

He trailed his oars and cocked his head and listened. "Could be," he said. "But I don't think so. I think there's a beaver dam in a creek back up in there. I think what we hear is the water coming over the top. I *know* that's what it is — there's a beaver house. It's in use, too. You can tell by all those bright new sticks piled there on top of the old."

"And there's your beaver," Worf said. "See him? He's just under that big, drooping willow."

I saw him — two wide-set eyes and a dark wet head — in a patch of shady water. Scholebo took a careful pull on the oars. But it wasn't careful enough. A big, flat, leathery tail came up and down in a slapping splash, and the beaver was gone.

"That's the fourth or fifth occupied beaver house I've seen today," Scholebo said. "And I've heard beaver moving in the sloughs. It looks to me like they're coming back real strong."

"I think they are," Worf said. "I hope so, anyway. It sure would be nice if they did." He turned to me. "I suppose you know that this was once the greatest beaver country in the West. General Ashley, Jim Bridger, Sir William Drummond Stewart, William Sublette, Jim Beckwourth, Jedediah Smith, all the famous mountain men — they all trapped along this part of the Green in the eighteen-twenties and thirties. All the old records and journals make it clear that they'd never seen anything like this river for beaver. It was so good it took them twenty years or more to clean it out."

"They tell me beaver makes pretty good eating," Scholebo said. "Beaver tail, I guess it is. I've never tried it, but if it's anything like most wild meat, I'd rather have a beefsteak."

"I like bear," Worf said. "I must say, though, that it's better if you don't have to stay in the house while it's cooking."

"Moose don't have such a good smell when it's cooking, either," Scholebo said. "To tell the truth, I don't care for either one. But maybe I'm wrong. All the moose I've ever eaten is big old bulls."

"I've eaten yearling bull moose and liked it fine," Worf said. "It was real good."

"You may be right," Scholebo said. "But I'd rather have a beefsteak."

A mule deer came out of the willows far up the beaver creek. I watched it browsing through the flowering bitter brush toward a high ridge densely grown with aspens. A patch of something white glittered from a break in the trees on the ridge. It was at least a hundred feet long and it looked at least ten feet high. It took me a moment to realize that it was a bank of lingering snow.

"I've seen drifts like that hang on right through the summer," Scholebo said. "The reason is they're placed so they don't get the sun but three or four hours a day. And then, of course, the thawing stops the minute the sun moves on or goes under a cloud or something. Also, it's pretty high up there. It must be close to nine thousand feet. Only a little higher and it freezes hard every night."

"There's an interesting sight you can see up in that high country some summers," Worf said. "The snow gets warm enough to support a growth of algae. I don't know the name of the algae, but it sure is an interesting sight. It turns the snowbanks pink."

"It can get real hot up there," Scholebo said.

"I know it can," Worf said. "Old Frémont came through these mountains in August of 1842, and his journal tells how he spent a night up there. It was up around Island Lake. He found a big, flat rock that had set in the sun all day, and he made his bed on that. Probably kept him warm all night long. Island Lake is part of Bridger now, and I hunted around there a couple of years ago and I think I found the rock he described. The sun lay on it just right, and it was nice and warm. It was hot."

The sound of running water came again. It came from a distance, but this time there was no mistaking it. I could already feel the current beginning to stir. There was another rapids up ahead.

"That's no beaver dam," Worf said.

"No," Scholebo said. "It sure as heck isn't. We're getting close to Kendall Warm Spring, and there's a stretch of pretty fast water just below where the Warm Spring Creek comes in. I think that's probably it." He turned to me. "Warm Spring is one of the big curiosities around here. If it wasn't so late, I'd suggest putting in and walking up for a look. The spring comes out of the rock in that ridge up there. But Jim Creek, where I plan to take out, is six or seven miles from here, and we haven't got that much time. Warm Spring is good and warm. It averages right around eighty degrees — winter and summer both. Winter is when you really notice it. It keeps the river free from ice for about a quarter of a mile downstream."

"There's another thing about Warm Spring," Worf said. "There's a species of dace in the springs that's unique. It's a little inch-long minnow that has adapted itself to that particular water — to that particular temperature and to certain elements, like sulphur, it contains. I understand it can't live anywhere else."

"I know it can't," Scholebo said. "The kids are always catching some of those minnows in a jar and taking them home for pets. But they very seldom get them home. The water cools off a little and they die."

We moved past the mouth of Warm Spring Creek. It looked like any creek. I leaned over the side and dipped my hand in the water. It felt as cold

145

as ever. But the river itself had changed again. Just below the surface of the water I could see the hump of a lurking boulder, and the sound of the rapids was loud and very near. The river cut to the left and back to the right and into a kind of canyon. The boat gave a sudden thrust. We dropped through a turmoil of whitecaps and burrowing eddies. A boulder twice the size of the boat loomed just ahead. Scholebo braked and pulled hard away to the right — and into the loom of another big boulder. I grabbed the gunwale and held my breath. The boat slammed up the side of the second boulder with a shriek that sounded like splintering wood. For an instant, we hung there, half out of water and half capsized. Then we slid back. I let out my breath. We were rocking and lurching and swinging broadside to the current, but we were dry and right side up. Scholebo brought the boat back under control, and we scraped down through an opening and into a stretch of fast but open water. I took a deep breath.

"You know," I said, "there was a moment there when I really thought —"

"You and me both," Worf said.

Scholebo smiled. "Me, too," he said.

We came out of the canyon and out of the rapids. The rolling sagebrush flats reappeared, and the sun seemed brighter and warmer. We passed the eroded remains of a ford. Then an old wooden bridge came into view. It crossed the river in a single span. A lonely dirt road came down to the bridge from the

▼▼▼

First Boat to King Island

THE ESKIMOS were waiting for us on the beach just beyond the boulder breakwater on the eastern outskirts of Nome. It was six o'clock in the evening, but the June sun was still high in the sky and the air was almost warm. Offshore a mile or two, the ice that had moved out in the night was white and clear on the horizon. We said good-bye to the friend who had driven us out from town, and unloaded our gear — boxes of food, seabags, sleeping bags, a portable Coleman stove, some photographic equipment — and carried it across the road and down the embankment and onto the beach. The beach was steep and stony, with dirty snow in the hollows and a heavy crust of ice at the edge of the water. The *umiak* was moored to the ice. It was an open dory made of walrus hide stretched over a wooden frame, and it looked to be about thirty feet long. The Eskimos — three men, three women, and three teen-age boys — were loading the boat from a pile of boxes and bundles and gasoline tins and oil drums and oars and ice lances and boat hooks and rifles. I counted a dozen rifles in the pile, and there were others already stacked in the bow of the boat. The Eskimos were King Island Eskimos. Their native place was a little island in the Bering Sea about a hundred miles northwest of Nome. They had spent the winter in Nome, and now that the ice was breaking up they were going back to King Island to take supplies to their friends and relatives there, to hunt for seal and walrus, and to collect for sale on the mainland the walrus-ivory carvings that the islanders had made during the winter. My companions — John Fuller, a teacher in a school for Eskimo children run by the Bureau of Indian Affairs, and Joseph Rychetnik, an outdoor photographer and a former Alaska state trooper — and I had arranged to go with them. Their boat would be the first to visit King Island since the ice had closed in last fall.

The Eskimos watched us coming down the beach. Some of them smiled, and one of the men waved. They all wore parkas with the hoods thrown back and dungarees, and most of them wore sealskin mukluk boots. The women wore flowered-cotton Mother Hubbards over their parkas. Two of the women, two of the boys, and one of the men wore glasses. The man who had waved came up to meet us. He was the boat captain, and his name was Vincent Kunnuk.

"No more to do," he said. "Everything is ready. We only wait for the old man."

Fuller nodded. He seemed to know what Kunnuk meant.

Kunnuk looked at me. "The old man has the experience," he said. "There is always an old man on a boat. He knows the weather and everything about the ice."

"I'm glad to hear it," Rychetnik said. "I made one patrol to King Island when I was on the police, and I got stuck there for over a week."

"I wonder if I know the old man," Fuller said.

"May be," Kunnuk said. "He is Pikonganna — Aloysius Pikonganna."

"Aloysius, eh?" Fuller said. "Good. Real good."

Kunnuk went back to the boat. We followed him down with our gear, and he showed us where to stow it. The boat was powered by two outboard motors — one at the stern and the other hung in a well a few feet forward. Two motors were no more than enough. They would have a lot of weight to move. The boat held nothing yet except gear, but it already sat low in the water. There wasn't much more than a foot of freeboard left.

A car stopped up on the road. The door opened and a little man on crutches got out. He had a rifle slung across his back. He called out something in Eskimo — a string of purrs and a sudden bark — and laughed and swung himself down the embankment.

"Now we go," Kunnuk said. "The old man is here. He goes on crutches all his life, but it makes no difference. He does everything a man can do."

The sea was a deep, translucent green and as flat as a village pond. We moved slowly away from the beach with only the stern motor working. Kunnuk sat at the helm. He kept the motor throttled down until we were clear of the shoals and shallows along the shore. Then he nodded to the man at the well, and the second motor coughed and stuttered and came alive, and the shore began to slide away. I watched the beach flatten out and the tumbledown houses across the road shrink down behind the embankment and the big brown mountainous hills rise up in the distance. Snow still lay on the tops of the hills and in their sheltered folds. The boat cut heavily away to the right, heading generally west, between the shore and the ice floes out to sea. I felt a breath of cooler air.

Aloysius Pikonganna sat in the bow on a plank laid across the gunwales. He had a pair of binoculars on a strap around his neck and a toothpick between his teeth. Below him, huddled in the shelter of a canvas windbreak, were the three women and the youngest boy. The boy wore a little pale-blue souvenir fedora, and on the front of the crown was a crayon scribble: *I want to hold your hand*. The other boys were packed in the stern with Kunnuk and the other men. Fuller, Rychetnik, and I sat amidships with the jumble of gear. I had a few inches of thwart to sit on and the iron curve of a fifty-gallon oil drum to rest my back against. Fuller was perched on the corner of an open box of pots and pans, and Rychetnik was sunk among his photographic equipment. But we were thickly padded with clothes. Rychetnik and I had on Bean hunting boots and two pairs of socks and Air Force survival pants and Eddie Bauer down-lined jackets over two heavy shirts and thermal underwear. Fuller wore an Eskimo uniform — fur parka, fur pants, and mukluk boots. He shifted on his box, and looked at me.

"Comfortable?" he asked.

"I'm fine," I said.

"I hope so," he said. "We've got at least fourteen hours of this ahead of us, you know."

"How about you?" I said.

"I'm O.K.," he said. "Besides, I'm used to it. This is just the way these cats are. They've always got room for one more."

"Just relax and enjoy it," Rychetnik said. "Be like me."

Pikonganna looked over his shoulder and raised a warning hand. There were ice floes in the sea ahead. The boat slowed down. Kunnuk stood up in the stern with his hand on the tiller and watched the drifting ice. Some of the floes were eight or ten feet in diameter, and some were twenty or thirty or fifty or more. All of them were four or five feet thick, but their edges were deeply undercut and they all were raddled with pools and puddles. We picked our way among them. A file of big black-and-white eider ducks came over the horizon. I watched them beating slowly along just clear of the water — and a dark shape moved on a floe far off to the left. It could only be a seal. One of the Eskimos let out a yell and grabbed up a rifle. But the seal was already gone. The Eskimo laughed and pulled the trigger anyway. The bullet whined away across the ice.

We came out from among the drifting floes and into a stretch of green open water. The boat began to move again. But after about ten minutes Pikon-ganna again held up his hand. There was more ice ahead. Everything in front of us was ice. The sea was a plain of shifting floes for as far as I could see. Kunnuk cut the motors, and we drifted up to the flank of one of the big floes. One of the men took a lance and chipped away the treacherous overhang and then jumped out on the floe. Pikonganna tossed him a line, and he stuck his lance in the ice and knotted the line around it. Another Eskimo followed him and secured the stern of the boat with another line and lance. Kunnuk came forward.

"Now we wait," he said. "But the ice is moving. It will open up pretty soon." He stepped on the gun-wale and onto the ice. "The women will make us some tea."

The women were already at work. They uncovered a Coleman stove and handed it out and set it up on the ice not far from the boat. While two of them got the stove started, the other woman got a tea-kettle and went off across the floe to a pool of melted ice. Rychetnik and Fuller and I stood on the ice, stamping the circulation back into our feet, and watched her fill the kettle from the pool.

"Do they make tea out of that?" I asked.

"Relax," Rychetnik said. "Salt-water ice isn't salty. The salt is expelled when salt water freezes. That's good water in that pool. I mean, it's fresh."

"It's potable," Fuller said. "Let's take a look at the ice. But be careful where you step. This rotten ice is full of potholes."

We walked down the floe. The ice was plainly moving. There was a lead of open water just ahead, and I could see that it was getting wider. The farther floe was pulling away in the grip of the tide. But the lead was still far from wide enough. I looked at my watch. It was twenty minutes past nine. Though the brightness had gone out of the sky, it was still full light. Everything was still fully visible — the hills and mountains on the mainland, a bread-loaf island in the distance, the drifting floes through which we had come. But the sun had moved down behind the mountains in the north, and it was only there that the sky had color. Overhead, it was dirty white, like a snowstorm sky, and the sky on the southern horizon was a cold, slaty blue. The mountains stood against a glory of pink and green and yellow.

When we got back to the boat, the Eskimos were gathered around a tarpaulin in front of the stove.

The tarpaulin was spread with food — a box of pilot crackers, a tin of butter, and a big square of whale blubber. The blubber looked like a block of cheese — pale-pink cheese with a thick black rind. We stopped at the boat and got a bag of sandwiches out of one of our boxes, and then joined the circle of Eskimos.

"It's moving, Vince," Fuller said. "It's opening up over there real fast."

"I know," Kunnuk said, and took a swallow of tea. "But we wait awhile. Have some tea." He spoke to the women in Eskimo, and picked up a fan-shaped knife with an ivory grip and cut off a slice of blubber. "Have some *muktuk?*"

Rychetnik smiled and shook his head.

"No, thanks, Vince," Fuller said. "Not right now."

Kunnuk laughed and looked at me. "This is the best *muktuk* — from the Bullhead whale. Black *muktuk.*"

I took the slice of *muktuk*. I sat down on the ice, and one of the women passed me a plastic cup of dark, steaming tea. I looked at the *muktuk*. The blubber didn't look like fat. It had a softer, more gelatinous look. I took a bite of it. It was very tender and almost tasteless. The only flavor was a very faint sweetness. There was one more bite of *muktuk* left. I ate it and washed it down with a gulp of tea. Then I opened my sandwich.

It was almost eleven o'clock when we finally left

the floe. The sky was still bright pink behind the mountains. We moved along a crooked lead of open water on one throttled-down motor. The floe on the left was piled with shattered slabs of pressure ice, sometimes to a height of four or five feet. Every now and then, the ice would give a kind of moan, and a big slab would slide into the water and the boat would lurch. Two of the Eskimos stood at the gunwales with lances and pushed the floating ice away. Pikonganna was standing at his lookout post. He looked at his watch, and turned and said something to one of the women. She reached under a pile of quilts and brought out a little plastic radio. It came alive with a thunder of Russian. Then a screech of static. Then a voice said, ". . . and partly cloudy tonight with widely scattered showers. Cloudy tomorrow. The present temperature in Nome is forty-two degrees." There was a moment of whistling silence, and then came the sound of guitars and a sob of Hawaiian music. The woman turned the radio off.

The lead began to broaden, and we were back in open water. The only big expanse of ice in sight was a shelf of anchored ice that stretched between the mainland and the distant bread-loaf island. Kunnuk came forward across the gear. He stepped over us and over the women and joined Pikonganna at the bow. They talked softly together for a couple of minutes. Then Kunnuk laughed and started back. He stopped where we sat, and balanced himself on the gunwale.

"The old man says we go around Sledge Island," he said. That was the bread-loaf island in the distance. "But after that — no sweat. No more ice."

I came out of a dull, uncomfortable doze. I was hunched against the flank of the oil drum, and I was stiff and cramped and cold. I sat up — and there was Sledge Island. It loomed hugely up no more than three hundred yards off the bow. There was a fringe of ice, a field of soggy snow, a rubble of boulders, and a brown grassy slope rising steeply to a brown grassy summit. My watch said five minutes to two. The sun was up from behind the mountains, but the sky was gray with cloud. We seemed to be making directly for the island. I looked at Fuller. Rychetnik was asleep face down between a seabag and a metal camera case, but Fuller was awake. He was sitting under the spread of his big parka hood, smoking a pipe.

"It looks like we're going to land," I said.

Fuller took the pipe out of his mouth. "Boat trouble," he said. "Vince says there's something wrong with one of the motors. He wants to stop and take a look at it."

Rychetnik sat up as we scraped alongside the shelf of anchored ice. "Hey," he said. "Where are we?"

"Sledge Island," I said.

"Sledge Island?" he said. "We're only at Sledge Island?"

"Relax," I said. "Relax and enjoy it."

When the boat was made fast, Kunnuk and one of the other men lifted the motor out of the well and began to take it apart. The trouble seemed to be in the feed line. I watched them for a minute. Then I followed the others through the field of snow to a ledge among the boulders, where the women had set up their stove. I sat down on a rock and gazed at them. They were boiling down snow for tea. I felt more than tired. I felt disoriented. The midnight daylight was confusing. After my sleep, it should have been morning. It gave me a very strange feeling.

Rychetnik touched me on the arm.

"Let's take our tea down the line a ways," he said. "Jack and I think it's time for a little depressant."

The idea of a drink at half past two in the morning was no stranger than anything else. I got up, and we sloshed through the snow to the sheltering lee of a boulder. Rychetnik handed each of us a little two-ounce bottle of Scotch, and we emptied them into our tea.

"It's better not to drink in front of the Eskimos," Rychetnik said. "It doesn't seem right unless you're going to pass the bottle around. And this is no place to do that."

"Good God, no," Fuller said. "I've lived and worked with Eskimos for quite a few years. As a matter of fact, I'm a first sergeant in the Eskimo

Scouts. I know them and I love them. I really love them. Those cats have to have something to survive in this environment, and they've got it. They've got every virtue. They're honest — they're completely honest — and they're loyal and they're generous and they're brave and they're always in good spirits. Nothing bothers them. But they can't drink. When they do, they get drunk. And when they get drunk, they go wild — they go absolutely wild."

We left Sledge Island with both motors working. I settled back in my oil-drum seat and listened to their steady, synchronized growl. The sea beyond the island was all open water. The only ice was off to the north, along the mainland shore. But the weather had also changed. The overcast was heavier now, and the breeze had sharpened, and the sea had faded from green to gray. I felt a drop of rain.

One of the women turned and caught my eye and smiled. She pointed toward the shore, and held up four fingers.

"Four years ago, we stay there one week," she said. "Bad weather. Then we stay three days at Sledge Island. More bad weather." She smiled again. "Was very bad trip."

"It sounds bad," I said.

She pointed again toward the shore. "Is called Pinguk," she said, and turned away.

I felt more drops of rain. There was a raincoat with a hood in my seabag. I felt around and found it and put it on and tied the hood under my chin. In the pocket was a pair of wool-lined rubber gloves, and I put them on, too. The rain burst into a spitting shower and then sank down to a long, cold drizzle. Rychetnik was asleep and snoring among his photographic gear, and Fuller sat humped on his box. Pikonganna stood on watch at the bow in a shiny translucent raincoat made of walrus intestines. I pulled up my legs and turned on my side and tried to fit myself against the curve of the oil drum. It wasn't very comfortable, but I was out of the wind and warm and dry. The last thing I remember was the rattle of the rain on my raincoat hood.

The boat was reeling and rolling, and it lurched me wide awake. It was almost six o'clock. I sat up and hung on to the thwart. We were rolling in a heavy chop. Rychetnik was also sitting up. He sat with one hand on the gunwale, bracing himself. It was still raining, and everything looked strangely dark. But it wasn't the darkness of night. Then I realized — it was fog. The boat gave a sickening roll. We were running broadside to the wind and wallowing in the trough of the waves. Rychetnik looked at me and smiled and shook his head.

"This is getting kind of hairy," he said.

"What's the matter?" I said.

"Aloysius says it's too rough to go on," he said. "Too rough and too foggy. We're turning around and heading in to shore."

Fuller leaned over my shoulder. "Too rough and

too foggy and only one motor," he said. "That motor conked out again."

"I wonder where we are," I said.

Fuller shrugged. "I don't know," he said. "My guess is somewhere off Cape Woolley."

"Where is that?" I said.

"Nowhere," he said. "It's just a name on the map."

"I know Cape Woolley," Rychetnik said. "I was up along there on my first assignment as a trooper. It was right around this time of year, too. I flew up from Nome with a bush pilot. As a matter of fact, it was Gene Farland. Three Eskimos had got drunk in Nome and gone out fishing in a skin boat and never came back. My job was to try to find them. Somebody said they had headed up this coast, so we took off. We flew along just above the beach — and pretty soon there was the boat. It was hanging up there in the driftwood. Then, a little farther on, we found the bodies. They weren't ten feet apart."

"What happened?" I said.

"There was a storm and they were drunk and the boat capsized and they went into the water," he said. "This is the Bering Sea. When you go into the water up here, that's the end of the story. You've had it."

"I don't know whether you've noticed," Fuller said, "but there aren't any life preservers on this boat."

The boat began to come around. It rocked and slipped and lumbered into the wind. Now that we were out of the trough, the heavy rolling stopped, and the boat sat a little steadier, but the head wind held us down to a bumpy crawl. We bumped through the chop for about an hour. It was a queer, empty twilit hour. There was nothing to see but the boat and the blowing rain and a few hundred feet of wild gray water vanishing into fog. It gave me an uneasy feeling. It was frightening to think that only half an inch of walrus hide lay between us and the clutch of that glacial water. But I was too tired and cramped and cold to really think about it.

A sheet of white ice emerged from the fog. It was shore ice anchored to a point of land. We moved along the flank of the ice, and the fog began to thin. The wind was blowing in offshore gusts, and it tore the thinning fog away in sudden streaks and patches. Land appeared beyond the ice. There was a narrow beach piled high with driftwood, a low embankment, and then a misty reach of tundra. A rhythmic whistling sounded overhead. I twisted my head and looked. It was a string of twenty or thirty big, dark-headed ducks swinging out to sea. Their size and the whistling made them goldeneyes. They dropped and braked and settled down on the water.

Kunnuk and Pikonganna exchanged a couple of shouts, and we edged closer in to shore. The shore ice shelf was deeply undercut, and its surface was ravaged with cracks and potholes. But apparently it would do — or would have to do. We came alongside, lifting and falling in the chop, and two of the men leaned out and hacked away the flimsy over-hang. Another man and one of the boys jumped out on the ice and held the boat fast with lines. Kunnuk came forward. His eyes were red, and his face looked drawn.

"Everybody out," he said. "This ice is no good. The old man says is too rotten to hold the boat. So we unload quick and get the boat up on the beach."

The man and the boy continued to hold the boat. The rest of us worked on the gear. We hauled the boxes and the bags and the cases and the rifles and the tins and the drums and the motors well up from the edge of the ice and covered them with some strips of tarpaulin. Then we went back to the boat and got a handhold on the bowline and dug in our heels. One of the women let out a wailing heave-ho yell, and we heaved. The bow of the boat lifted and hung, and then slid up on the ice. We braced ourselves, and the woman yelled again: "Hooooo-*huke!*" We heaved again. One of the Eskimos stepped through a pot-hole up to his thigh, and I slipped and sat down hard on the ice, but the boat came up another five or six feet. Another heave brought all but the stern of it clear of the water, and after that it was easier. With some of us pulling and the rest pushing, the boat slid over the soggy ice like a sled. There was no need now for the women to help. They got their stove and some other supplies and then went on across the ice and up the beach to the tundra. By the time we got there with the boat, the women had collected a supply of driftwood branches and logs, and even trees, and had a big fire going. We careened the boat a few feet from the fire and propped it up on its side with the oars and boat hooks. It made an excellent windbreak and a kind of shelter from the rain.

We stood around the fire and warmed ourselves and caught our breath. The wind tore at the fire, and the flames leaped and twisted and darted in all directions, and my face was scorched but my feet stayed cold. It was a hot and furious fire. It took a lot of driftwood to keep it going, and the wood that the women had collected went fast. It was the deadest driftwood I had ever seen. Years of weathering on this desert beach had dried it to papery husks, and it burned almost like paper. When the woodpile was down to a few sticks and branches, Rychetnik and I volunteered to bring in another supply. It was plentiful enough. There was driftwood heaped head high at the high-water mark along the beach as far as I could see. It must have been accumulating there forever. We made a dozen trips and brought back a dozen logs — big, barkless silver-gray logs that weighed practically nothing. As we dropped our last load, Fuller came struggling up from the ice with a box and a bag of perishables. The women had their stove set up, and they were making tea and boiling a pot of mush. Rychetnik looked at them and then at his watch.

"Hey," he said. "It's eight o'clock. What are *we* going to do about breakfast?"

"Whatever you say," Fuller said. "But I didn't get any sleep last night and I'm really not too hungry."

"Neither am I," I said.

"Besides," Fuller said, "I'm not real eager to break out the stove right now and do a lot of cooking and washing up and getting packed again. It wouldn't be worth the trouble. My guess is this weather is going to clear, and I know these cats. They'll be wanting to take right off."

"But what about breakfast?" Rychetnik said.

"I brought up the rest of the sandwiches," Fuller said. "And we've got some cans of chocolate milk."

Fuller was right about the weather. The rain had stopped by the time we finished breakfast, and the clouds were breaking up. There were patches of bright sky overhead, and the air was bright and clear. Even the wind had dropped. It looked like a beautiful day, but we wouldn't be leaving soon. The sea was still running high and white. Fuller dragged himself away from the fire and lay down in the shelter of the boat. Almost at once, he was snoring. I was tired, but the change in the weather made me restless. Rychetnik was engrossed in his cameras. I got up and walked around the boat and out onto the tundra.

The tundra stretched endlessly away to the north and south, and far to the east, a smoky gray on the blue horizon, were mountains. It was an enormous, empty plain. There were no trees, no bushes, no grass. There were only weedy hummocks and pockets of bog and trickling, ice-water brooks. Some of the hollows were still drifted over with snow. I skirted a bog and stepped over a brook, and a bird flew up from almost under my foot. It was followed by another. They were tawny, long-billed birds — snipe. A few minutes later, I flushed a phalarope. The tundra wasn't as empty as it looked. There were shrieks and whistles and drumming wings at almost every step I took. I flushed more snipe and phalaropes, and also sandpipers and plovers and ptarmigan. The ptarmigan had a shabby look. Their plumage was still a confusion of winter white and summer brown. Once, in the distance, I saw a flight of sandhill cranes, and there were many strings of ducks and geese. The geese were mostly snow geese, but there were also emperor geese and brant. The sun came suddenly out. It blazed down like a tropical sun. I unfastened my padded jacket, and then took it off. It was actually hot. I sat down on a hummock and folded my jacket into a pillow and lay back. The hummock was matted with lingenberry vines and tiny creeping willow, and it made a soft and springy bed. I closed my eyes and enjoyed the feel of the sun on my face.

I woke up cold and shivering. The sun was gone and the fog was back, and it took me a moment to remember where I was. I put on my jacket and started back to the camp. My head was still thick

with sleep. I stopped at a brook and squatted down
and splashed some water on my face. That finished
waking me up. I went on, stepping and stretching and
hopping from hummock to hummock. The fog made
everything seem very still. The mountains had disappeared in the fog, but I could see the camp across the
tundra. A small white tent now stood not far from
the driftwood fire. Several men were gathered at the
bow of the upturned boat. One of them was Rychetnik. I waved, and he came out to meet me. He was
grinning.

"We'll never get off this beach," he said.

"Not with this fog," I said.

"I don't mean only the weather," he said.

"Now what?" I said.

"More boat trouble," he said. "One of the Eskimos was sacked out under the boat, and he happened
to look up — and what do you think he saw?"

"What?" I said.

"Daylight," he said. "There was a hole in the
bottom of the boat about the size of a dime. Vince
and Sam Mogg are patching it up. They think it
probably happened when we were dragging the boat
up over the driftwood."

"What about that conked-out motor?" I said.

"I think they've finally got that fixed," he said.
"But don't start getting any ideas. There's something wrong with the other motor now. It needs a
shear pin on the propeller shaft. They're going to fix
that this afternoon."

"Do you have any more of those little bottles you had last night?" I said.

Rychetnik laughed. "No," he said. "But I've got a big one."

I followed him around the boat and around the fire and around behind the Eskimo tent. Fuller was there, sitting on a log in front of our portable stove and searching through a box of groceries. He looked refreshed by his nap, and resigned to a stay on the beach. I filled a pan with water from the nearest snow-melt brook, and Fuller found some paper cups, and Rychetnik got out a fifth of Scotch. We sat around the stove and drank our drinks. The Scotch was good with the cold snow water, and it made the fog and the beach and the miles of tundra seem less bleak. Then Fuller cooked us a lunch of bacon and eggs. It was the first hot food I had eaten in almost twenty-four hours, and nothing ever tasted any better. We finished off with bread and butter and strawberry preserves and a pot of strong boiled coffee.

We spent the afternoon hauling driftwood for the fire. The Eskimo tent had been raised for the women, and we could hear them talking and laughing inside whenever we stopped at the fire to rest and warm ourselves. We also worked to the sound of shooting. The Eskimo boys roamed up and down the beach with .22 rifles, and they shot at anything that made a target — a driftwood stump, a raft of ducks far out to sea, a flight of mile-high geese. Kunnuk sat alone in the shelter of the upturned boat with a cigarette in his mouth and filed and shaped a nail into a new shear pin. When he finished, he walked down and stood on the edge of the beach and looked at the water. The next time I came back to the fire, he was sitting there with the portable radio in his lap. I sat down beside him. We listened to a snatch of Siberian Russian and the end of a talk about getting back to the Bible. A hillbilly tenor sang "Does He Love You Like I Do?" Then a voice said: "This is radio station KICY, in Nome, Alaska. The time is six o'clock. Here is the weather forecast for Nome and vicinity: Fair and cold tonight. Fair and warmer tomorrow. The present temperature in Nome is thirty-three degrees."

Kunnuk turned off the radio. "Good weather coming," he said. "Maybe we leave soon. Maybe by midnight."

But the fog hung on. At nine o'clock, it looked thicker than ever. I doubted that we would be leaving by midnight, and I didn't care. I hardly cared if we ever left. Work and the weather and a drink of Scotch had given me a big appetite, and I had eaten a big dinner of reindeer steak, macaroni and cheese, canned peaches, cookies, and coffee. All I wanted to do was sleep. Someone would wake me before we left. If we left. I found a corner deep under the boat and took off my boots and my jacket and my heavy survival pants and unrolled my sleeping bag and crawled in. Something poked into the small of my back. There was a stick or something under my sleeping bag. I tried to squirm it away, and it moved an inch or two. That wasn't enough. I would have to climb out and move the bag. But instead I fell asleep.

I slept all night. I awoke to a crying and croaking and whistling of birds. It was half past five. There was frost on the ground, and the air was cold, but the sea looked calm, and the sun was shining in a wide blue sky. The fog was completely gone. I sat up. Kunnuk was propped on his elbow in a sleeping bag on my left.

"We make it today," he said. "Look!" He handed me a pair of binoculars and pointed out to sea. "You can see King Island."

I looked, but I couldn't see it.

"Maybe I know better where to look," he said. "I was born there."

I got into my clothes and rolled up my sleeping bag. Underneath it was the end of one of the boat lines. I stooped out from under the boat and into the bright sunlight. Most of the others were already up. The women were boiling another big pot of mush. I washed my face in the snow-melt brook. The water felt even colder than it had the day before. It was so cold it made my nose ache. I was starting back when Rychetnik came up to get some water for breakfast, and we walked back together. The stove was going, and Fuller, in a bright-red hunting shirt, was peeling bacon into a frying pan. Then, while Rychetnik got the coffee started and I got out some cups and plates and knives and forks and spoons, he stirred up a bowl of pancake batter. He fried the pancakes in the bacon pan, and we ate them with butter and strawberry preserves.

We finished breakfast at a little after six, and a few minutes later the Eskimos began to break camp. The women did the packing. Kunnuk called us over to help the men with the boat. We rolled it back on its keel and swung it around and dragged it down and across the ice and let it into the water. The glare of the sun on the frosty ice was dazzling. Two of the boys held the boat against the edge of the ice, and we went back and got our gear. The ground where the women's tent had been was littered with bones and cigarette butts. Aloysius Pikonganna directed the loading of the boat. The arrangement was somewhat different from that at Nome. It was planned for safe and easy shooting if we happened to get a shot at a seal. Rychetnik and Fuller and I shared the forward thwart again, but the gear was all piled amidships and the women and two of the boys were also settled there. The other boy and a man called Norbert took over the motors, with Norbert doing the steering. Kunnuk and Sam Mogg joined Pikonganna in the bow with the guns. We pushed away from the shore, and I looked over the side of the boat. The water was a yellowy green and so clear that I could see the bottom, five or six feet below. The bottom was stone — big slabs of granite worn smooth by grinding ice. It was as smooth and flat and bare as a pavement.

The motors started up, first the one at the stern and then the other, and the boat began to move. The women huddled closer together. They bowed their heads and made the sign of the cross, and their lips moved silently in prayer. Then they sat back, and two of them lighted cigarettes. We left the last of the shore ice and came out into open water and into an easy swell. Yesterday's chop had gone with the fog. An acre of rafting eider ducks exploded off to the right. I watched the big birds beating slowly in to shore. The shore looked just as it had when we saw it on Thursday morning. There was no sign that any-one had ever camped there. Kunnuk turned and looked back down the boat. He was smiling, with a cigarette in his mouth, and sparks of sunlight glinted on his glasses.

"Everybody sleep good?" he said.

The women nodded and the boys grinned and Norbert yelled something in Eskimo. Everybody laughed.

"Good," Kunnuk said. "Now we got good weather. Now we travel."

Sam Mogg caught my eye.

"We got Sears, Roebuck weather," he said.

"What?" I said.

"Sears, Roebuck weather," he said. "I ordered it."

The radio came suddenly on. A familiar voice said, ". . . seven o'clock, and the present tempera-ture in Nome is forty-four degrees. The wind is

northeast at fourteen. The forecast is for fair and
warmer today, tonight, and tomorrow." In spite of
the sun, it was cold on the water. I could feel the
forecast wind. I zipped up my jacket and put on my
gloves and listened to an operatic tenor singing "I
Love to Laugh." He sounded very far away. When
he laughed ("Ha-ha, hee-hee"), he sounded even remoter.

King Island came faintly into sight at about eight-
thirty. It was just a cloud on the western horizon. I
got out a pair of binoculars and fixed them on the
cloud. The cloud became a bigger and darker cloud,
but it was still no more than a cloud. Then it began
to grow. It darkened and broadened and lifted
against the sky. By nine o'clock, the cloud was visibly
an island. It continued to grow, and to change.
Through the binoculars I watched it shift from a little gray lift of land to a rocky mountain rising
steeply from the sea.

The woman who had spoken to me before leaned
forward. She was an elderly woman with a big,
square face framed in her parka hood.

"King Island," she said. "You see?"

I nodded. "It looks like a mountain," I said.

"Ukivok is Eskimo name," she said. "Not King
Island. Eskimo call it Ukivok."

"Ukivok," I said. "What does that mean in Eskimo?"

"We go up on top Ukivok," she said. "We go

high up and pick green flower. Many green flower grow on top Ukivok now."

"What is green flower?" I said.

"Is good," she said. "Is like salad."

Floating ice began to appear up ahead. A flight of murre swung low across our bow, and in the distance a kittiwake soared. King Island rose higher and higher. I watched it through the binoculars. It looked to be about two miles long, and it really was a mountain. Its sides were weathered into crags and pinnacles, and they rose abruptly from a beach of anchored ice to a saddle summit that was still partly covered with snow and at least a thousand feet high. It seemed impossible that anyone could live there.

I turned to the woman behind me. "Where do the people live on Ukivok?" I said. "Where is the village?"

"Ukivok is name of village," she said. "Island and village is same name."

"Where is Ukivok village?" I said.

She smiled and shook her head. "Not this side," she said. "Too much mountain. On other side."

Fuller gave me a nudge. "Walrus," he said, and pointed off to the left.

I put up the binoculars again. I saw them almost at once — a row of six or eight enormous creatures sitting erect on an isolated floe. They were reddish brown, with big sloping shoulders and little round heads and drooping two-foot tusks. They had a prehistoric look. They also looked strangely human.

sharp bills. Sitting erect on the ice, they even looked like penguins.

Pikonganna suddenly stiffened, and then sank slowly down on his plank. It was an alerting movement. Everybody tensed.

"*Ooguruk*," he said, and pointed.

About a hundred and fifty yards to the right, a big, silvery bearded seal lay basking on a floating floe. It hadn't seen or heard us yet. Norbert cut the motors and we drifted silently toward the ice. Nobody spoke. The most accessible rifle of adequate caliber was a Remington .30/06, and the man closest to it was Fuller. It was Rychetnik's rifle, and he motioned to Fuller to take it. Nobody moved. Fuller swung the gun to his shoulder, steadied himself, and fired. A flight of murre veered loudly away. The seal gave a start, and lay still.

The boat nudged up to the floe, and Kunnuk vaulted over the gunwale and onto the ice. He had a revolver in his hand. Sam Mogg and Fuller jumped ashore and trotted after Kunnuk. Rychetnik and I got out on the ice and watched them. Kunnuk was the first to reach the seal. Apparently, it was still alive. He squatted down and shot it in the head. He put the revolver away and took out a hunting knife and cut two belt-loop slits in the skin just above the eyes. Sam Mogg and Fuller came sliding up, and Mogg threw Kunnuk a length of rope. Kunnuk threaded the rope through the belt-loop slits and made it fast, and then he and Mogg and Fuller dragged the seal across the floe to the boat. The seal was a young female. It was about six feet long and it weighed at least four hundred pounds, and Kunnuk and Fuller and Mogg were sweating when they got it up to the boat. They were grinning, too. Everybody was grinning, and Mogg slapped Fuller on the back. When Kunnuk and Fuller and Mogg had caught their breath, they rolled the seal over on its back, and Kunnuk got out his knife again and gutted and cleaned it. Then they hoisted the carcass over the gunwale and into the bow. The fur looked suddenly different. The brilliant silver luster had begun to fade. By the time we were ready to leave, it was a dingy, leaden gray.

We moved along the lakelike lead. The wind and the tide were shifting the ice, and the lead grew wider and more open. There was open water now all the way to the looming cliffs. I stood up. There was open water everywhere ahead. An open lagoon stretched for two or three hundred yards between the shelf of anchored ice and the foot of the cliffs, and it seemed to encircle the island. We moved across the open water and into the shadow of the cliffs. Then, at a signal from Kunnuk, Norbert swung the boat to the left. We headed down the eastern face of the island. I looked up at the towering crags and pinnacles. Every ledge was a rookery.

The rocks were alive with perching murre and kitti-wakes, and gulls and auklets and cormorants and puffins and terns.

Kunnuk turned around. He had his revolver in his hand. "You like to see some birds?" he said, and pointed the revolver overhead. "Just watch — I show you something."

He fired two shots, and then a third. The revolver was only a .22, but against the sounding board of water and rock it sounded like a bomb. It sounded like a hundred bombs. The shots went echoing up and down the face of the island, and a cloud of birds came screaming off the cliffs. They flew screaming over our heads and across the lagoon to the outer ice and then veered around and came streaming back. They came off the cliffs and over the water in waves — hundreds, thousands, tens of thousands of birds. It was impossible to even guess at the number.

The elderly woman leaned over my shoulder. "Ukivok is good place for eggs," she said. "All kinds of eggs." She smiled at me. "Very good to eat."

We sailed down the lagoon in a turbulence of birds. Many of them were birds that had never seen a man or a boat or heard a shot before, and it took them a long time to settle down again. The lagoon was irregularly shaped. Because of the broken line of the shifting outer ice, it was sometimes as wide as a lake and sometimes no more than a river. We followed it across a lake and through a little river and into another lake. I heard the motors cut off and felt the boat begin to drift. Pikonganna and Kunnuk were standing together on the lookout plank, and Sam Mogg and Rychetnik and Fuller were on their feet. Even Norbert was standing. I stood up, too. The lake we were in was the end of the lagoon.

Kunnuk came down off the plank. "O.K.," he said. "We go back. We go round the other way."

We all sat down. The motors started up, and the boat swung around, and we headed back up the lagoon. The boat suddenly slowed. Kunnuk was back on the lookout plank with Pikonganna, and Mogg was standing below them peering out between their legs. I couldn't tell what they were looking at. I didn't see anything unusual. We were approaching the upper end of the lake, and it looked much like the other end. And then I realized. The outer ice was moving in on some shift of wind or tide, and the little riverlike passage through which we had come had almost disappeared. The passage was about two hundred feet long, and ten or fifteen minutes ago it had been a good hundred feet wide. It now was hardly twenty.

The boat began to move again. Pikonganna and Kunnuk had come to some decision. We made our way across the last of the lake to the head of the passage. The passage had an ugly look. There was a ten-foot embankment of glassy ice on the island side, and the outer ice was pitted with holes and piled with pressure ridges, and it was moving fast. I could see it closing in. Rychetnik gave a kind of grunt.

"I don't like this very much," he said. "I don't think I like it at all. You know what this boat is made out of. If we get caught between the ice in there . . ."

"I don't like it, either," I said. "But I guess there isn't much choice."

"These cats know what they're doing," Fuller said. "I've never seen them take a chance they didn't have to."

The boat edged into the passage. The water was thick with chips and chunks of floating ice. We moved carefully between the embankment of anchored ice and the moving floe on one throttled-down motor. Norbert kept the boat inching along just off the lip of the floe, away from the height and bulk of the ice embankment, but every time I looked, the ice seemed higher and closer. I could already feel the cold of its breath. Kunnuk reached out with an ice lance and jabbed at the edge of the floe. He jabbed again, hard, and a slab of ice came loose and slid slowly into the water. The boy at the stern with Norbert poked it safely past the boat with an oar. It was rotten ice. The whole rim of the floe was rotten ice.

Kunnuk said something in Eskimo, and stepped up on the gunwale and jumped out on the floe. Mogg and Fuller followed him over, and Rychetnik and the boy at the stern followed them. They all had lances or boat hooks, and they spread out along the floe and began hacking at the rim of rotten ice. They worked just ahead of the inching boat, and Pikonganna hung

over the bow with an oar and guided the slabs of
floating ice to the island side of the passage. I found
another oar and kept the ice moving and clear of the
boat. Some of the slabs were the size of boulders,
and it took all my strength and weight hanging on
the oar to push them off and away. But I kept them
moving, and the boat was also moving, and finally I
raised my head and looked out over Pikonganna's
shoulder and there was the end of the passage and a
blue expanse of open water. Norbert shouted, and
the women gave a quavering wail. We were through.

We went back up the eastern face of the island
and around the northern end and down the western side. Everybody was talking and laughing. There
was no ice anywhere on the western side except along
the shore, but the island was the same. There were
the same gray cliffs, the same patches of yellow
lichen, the same thousands of screaming birds. There
was no sign of a village, and no place where a village
might even conceivably be built. So the village was
down at the southern end of the island. We still had
some distance to go. I looked at my watch, and I
could hardly believe it. It had been nine hours since
we stopped for lunch. It was almost nine o'clock.

Rychetnik had been dozing in the evening sun.
He sat up and shook himself. "I'm getting kind of
hungry," he said. "As a matter of fact, I'm starved."

"I've been thinking about our dinner," Fuller
said. "I thought the first night on King Island we

ought to have something real special. Anybody got any suggestions?"

"I suggest we all go down to the Four Seasons," Rychetnik said.

"We've got a ham," Fuller said. "It's one of those Polish hams. I guess we'll have that, and maybe some spaghetti."

"And a drink," I said.

"Don't worry about that," Rychetnik said.

The village was well around on the southern tip of the island. It was built on the slope of a chute of landslidden rocks. It hung on the slope about three hundred feet above a beach of ice and tumbled boulders, and it consisted of eighteen or twenty houses. The houses were wooden shacks with tarpaper roofs, and they were stepped out from the slope on tall wooden stilts. Scaffolding walks and ladderlike steps connected the houses, and a long flight of steps led down to the boulder beach.

"It looks even hairier closer up," Rychetnik said. "But I guess it's safe enough. The house we're going to stay in is the schoolhouse — what used to be the schoolhouse. The teacher left about ten years ago. It's the house with all those windows up there at the head of the steps. That's where I stayed when I was here before. It isn't any Hilton, but it's got four walls and a roof and some chairs to sit on and a table. It won't be too bad."

The boat turned in toward the shore, and I watched the village coming clearer. It was hard to think of it as an Eskimo village. It looked remoter than that. It looked Tibetan. A man came out on the balcony of one of the upper houses. There was a green and red and purple patchwork quilt hung over the railing to air. The man watched us for a moment. Then he raised both hands high over his head and waved. Pikonganna waved back. He was grinning from ear to ear. He reached down and slapped Kunnuk on the back.

"Home sweet home, boy," he said. "There's no place like home."

Kunnuk smiled and nodded. "That's right," he said.

▼▼▼

The Witness Tree

A tree's a tree — how many more do you need to look at?

— RONALD REAGAN

▲▲▲

THE HIGHWAY ran on and on between two walls of trees. The trees were mainly white oak and beech and loblolly pine, with here and there a Southern magnolia, and they rose from the roadside sixty, eighty, a hundred feet into the hot blue morning sky. This was the Big Thicket of East Texas. It was the remains of a bog-and-bayou wilderness that once — before sawmills and oil wells and pipelines and subdivisions and water-ski resorts — spread over more than three million acres of land in the counties of Polk, Tyler, Hardin, and Liberty. At the urging of local conservationists, the National Park Service had recently proposed that some thirty-five thousand acres of this remainder be preserved as a National Monument, and we — Ernest Borgman, superintendent of Padre Island National Seashore, at Corpus Christi, and I — had driven up to spend a day in that part of the Thicket.

The wall of woods moved back from the highway, and an old frame house appeared on the left, and then, on the right, a field of grazing cattle with cattle egrets following underfoot. At the edge of the field was a sign: SARATOGA. Saratoga (pop. 806), a village founded by a nostalgic upstate New Yorker, lies close to the heart of the Big Thicket, and it was here that we had arranged to pick up our guide, a local naturalist named Lance Rosier. The highway became a street. There was a Texaco station on one side of the street and a Fina station on the other. Then came a block of houses, and then a block of one-story buildings with covered sidewalks: *Crouch Coca-Cola Gro., Wimpy's Carnation Fresh Milk Gro. & Mkt., Crawford's Have-a-Pepsi Café,* a barbershop with a wooden barber pole, a Gulf station, a brick post office. Rosier was waiting for us on a bench in front of the post office. He was a small man with a big nose and big ears, and he had on a faded blue work shirt and a little cotton golf hat. Borgman pulled in to the curb, and Rosier got up and came across to the car. He looked to be about seventy. He gave us each a limp, country handshake, and got into the back seat and sat there with his hands folded in his lap.

"Well, Lance?" Borgman said.

"Sir?" Rosier said.

"Where to?" Borgman said. "Where do we start?"

"Do you know the old Ghost Road?" Rosier said.

"I've heard of it," Borgman said. He swung the car around, and we headed back out of town. "It's on the way to Big Sandy and Tight-Eye and all up there."

"Yes, sir," Rosier said. "Turn right, please."

We turned off the highway and onto a narrow sandy road. It ran between fields of grazing cattle and greening corn for half a mile, and then the woods rose up and we were back in the Thicket. The woods were deep and dense and dark, and there was standing water under most of the trees. In the water along the roadside were spiky clumps of scrub palmetto. Up ahead, a buzzard hung over the road. It was a spooky-looking place.

"This must be the Ghost Road," I said.

"Yes, sir," Rosier said. "It is. And do you notice how straight it runs? It runs as straight as an arrow for nine miles — all the way to Bragg. Bragg is a ghost now, too. This used to be a branch line of the Gulf, Colorado & Santa Fe Railway. They tore up the tracks in 1934. But that's only partly why they call this the Ghost Road. There's supposed to be a ghost in here. A man was jacking deer in here one night, and he was drinking and he got himself drunk. So he lay down on the railroad tracks to rest. He was still laying there when the train come along, and it cut off his head. The ghost is his lantern. People still see it burning here at night."

"Have you ever seen it, Lance?" Borgman said.

"No, sir," Rosier said. "Now, do you notice that right along here you don't see any hardwood? The lumber company — one of them — sprayed about seven thousand acres to kill off the hardwood and get a pure stand of pine for lumber. It was a hormone spray, and they did it from a helicopter. That was about three years ago. So you don't see any hardwood at all. Or any birds, either."

We drove on down an endless aisle of loblolly pine. After a couple of miles, the woods deepened and darkened, and another buzzard hung over the road. We were out of the pine desolation. Rosier leaned forward. There was something moving on the road ahead. The movement took form — a big brown sow and eight tumbling little pigs. But a glimpse was all I got. There was another commotion, and they all were gone.

Rosier laughed. "Now you know we're out of the sprayed area," he said. "Those wild pigs are a sure sign. They live on acorns. They live right well, too. They can get up to three and four hundred pounds. There are all kinds of animals gone feral in the Thicket. There are pigs like those, and cats and goats, and even some cattle. And about a year ago a man I know got tired of a herd of jackasses he had and he turned them loose in here. I believe there were twenty-six of them. They're all in here somewhere."

"What about real wild animals?" I said.

"Yes, sir," he said. "We have those, too. Including rattlesnakes and copperheads and water moccasins. We've got deer and coons and possums and skunks and otters and foxes and flying squirrels and bobcats and cougars, and there used to be some jaguars. I know there are still some bear — black bear. I've seen them. And there are plenty of armadillos. I don't know about alligators. I think the poachers have just about killed them all. But there may be a few still left in places where even those fellows don't like to go."

"Don't forget the ivorybill, Lance," Borgman said.

"The ivory-billed woodpecker?" I said. "I thought that was supposed to be extinct."

"Yes, sir," Rosier said. "That's what everybody thought. But it isn't. There are still a few of them here in the Thicket. That's one reason why I'd like to see the Monument go through. You have to go deep to find them, though. The first confirmed sighting in many years was a couple of years ago, and there have been several more since then. They tell about one fellow that saw one, and to prove it he shot it and brought it in. I don't know how true that is."

"No," Borgman said. "But I do know there are people like that."

The Ghost Road came out on a gravel highway. Beyond the highway was the main line of the Gulf, Colorado & Santa Fe, and on a siding were six flatcars loaded with loblolly logs. The logs were the length of telephone poles and at least two feet in diameter. Beyond the railroad tracks the Thicket began again.

"Turn left, please," Rosier said. He cleared his throat. "You know, this is right nice. I'm right happy to go out with you fellows today. I always like to get back in the Thicket. It's where I've spent most of my life. I started when I was just a boy. I never was big enough to play ball or anything, so I took to going back in the Thicket. I wanted to learn what was there — what was growing there. The other fellows, they called me crazy. They called me sissy, too. That's the way it was in those days. If a man even planted a rosebush in his front yard they called him henpecked. But I didn't pay any mind to that. I used to leave home — I was living with my auntie then — with a bag for specimens and a sweet potato in my pocket for lunch, and spend the day in the Thicket. I liked wild flowers, but I didn't know but a very few. There weren't any books — any field guides — in those days. What I did was this. When I found a flower I didn't know, I'd wrap it up and send it off to one of the colleges, and by and by they would write me back and give me the name — both names — for it. There are over a thousand species of flowering plants in the Thicket, and I learned them all, and that's the way I did it. I learned them the hard way."

"The best way," Borgman said.

"Yes, sir," Rosier said. "I think so, too. Now, if you'll turn right, please — at that little dirt road up there. I want to show you one of the most historic spots in East Texas. Then we'll go on to Big Sandy."

The dirt road took us across the railroad tracks and into another deep woods. A cardinal blazed out of the trees and down the edge of the road. But that was only the first one. This was a haven for cardinals. In not much more than a mile, I counted eleven of them. It was also a garden of wild flowers. The roadside grass was bright with crimson clover and blue vervain and yellow buttercups. Even the air was sweet with some rich and blossomy scent. I looked back at Rosier.

"Hawthorn," he said.

We crossed a little brown creek on a bridge of old crossties. A column of dust rose up ahead, and we came up behind a heavy truck.

"That looks like a well-pulling rig," Borgman said.

"Yes, sir," Rosier said. "They've got a lot of oil fields around in here, and he's probably going in to pull out some wells that have given out and gone dry. You'll see where he's going directly. You can't very well miss it. And if you listen you can hear a power saw over yonder. That's some of what's happening to the Big Thicket. They tell me the Thicket is going at the rate of fifty acres a day."

We dropped back out of the dust and followed the truck at a distance. We followed it for a couple of miles. Then the road took a turn, and when we came around the bend the truck was gone. And so were the woods. On both sides of the road lay a waste of mud and puddles and rotting stumps and a few palmetto saplings. This was the remains of an oil field. It covered forty or fifty acres, and off to the right, through a screen of skeleton trees, I could see the scar of a second field and the truck moving on toward another.

"What did all that?" I said. "Spilled oil?"

"No, sir," Rosier said. "They don't waste anything that valuable. It's the salt water they have to pump out of the wells that does the damage. It does a right good job, too. They abandoned this field at least five years ago."

"It's gone," Borgman said.

I looked at the poisoned land. It couldn't be helped: this was the look of the twentieth century. I supposed it couldn't be helped. But it made me feel sick, and I was thankful when the woods sprang up from the ruins and we were back again in the green of the Thicket.

Rosier leaned forward. "Here we are," he said. "Pull over, please — up there by that big sweet gum. This is the history I want to show you. I'm going to take you back in the woods and show you the Keyser Burnout."

Borgman pulled off the road and under the big gum tree. We got out, and Rosier led the way across the road and onto an overgrown wagon-track trail.

The trees arched and mingled overhead, and some of them were hung with pink-flowered honeysuckle. It was hot and damp and dim and still, and there were mosquitoes everywhere. And birds. The birds were hidden in the trees, but I could hear them calling — a crow, a cardinal, a white-eyed vireo, a warbler of some kind, a Carolina wren.

"The Keyser Burnout goes back to the War Between the States," Rosier said. "The first residents of the Big Thicket were what they called jayhawkers. They were draft evaders. They were people who didn't own no slaves, so they didn't see no reason to fight, and to keep from being drafted they hid out in here. There were whole families of them. I don't know exactly how many. Different people tell it different. But there must have been anyway two hundred. They lived very careful. They split up into two groups, and each group had its own well, and they came and went through the Thicket without even breaking a twig. But they lived right well. They lived on game and wild honey. They didn't need for anything but coffee and tobacco, and they traded game for that. The government was against them, of course, and finally it sent a man named Captain Keyser up from Galveston to root them out. He come up the Trinity River with his troops and sent word into the Thicket that they either give up or he would burn them out. The jayhawkers wouldn't give up, but there are two different stories about what happened next. One story is that when Captain Keyser set the

woods on fire, the jayhawkers all run off and he
never did find them. The other story is that they all
burned up in the fire. The only thing I ever heard
people agree on about the jayhawkers was where
Mr. Lilly was shot. Mr. Lilly wasn't a jayhawker,
but he was out in the Thicket hunting one day, and
Captain Keyser's soldiers mistook him for one, and
they shot him. The bullet hit him right where his gal-
luses crossed."

"He must have been running away," Borgman
said.

"Yes, sir," Rosier said. "I reckon he was
scared." He slapped a mosquito. "And this is where
the Keyser Burnout starts. You notice here on the
right the woods is all slash pine. That's where the
Burnout was. It's all pine for over two hundred
acres."

There was a crossroads up ahead, and Borgman
slowed the car. Just beyond the crossing, in a clearing on the left, was a little white store with a big red
sign: *Williams Dr Pepper Gro*. A dirt track led
around the store and across the clearing and into the
woods behind. A man on a horse came out of the
woods. But it wasn't a horse. He was riding a sad-
dled mule.

"This is Segno," Rosier said. "If you want to see
Big Sandy Creek, we can park right here and walk in.
It isn't but a couple of miles."

We left the car near the store and walked up the track. It climbed through the woods and around the slope of a hill to an open grove of big magnolia trees. There was a long, low building under the trees with a corrugated-iron roof and a sign above the door: *Welcome to Magnolia Hill Assembly of God Church.* On one side of the church were three long, rickety picnic tables.

"My God," Borgman said. "Look at those old tables. They really bring back memories."

"They used to have a saying," Rosier said. " 'Dinner on the ground, preaching all around.' "

"I never heard that," Borgman said. "But that sure is the way it was."

We walked on beyond the church and down past a burying ground. Pink phlox and bluebonnets were growing together between the gravestones, and I could see bees working among the flowers. There was still wild honey in the Thicket. Magnolia Hill was the end of the track. Beyond the burying ground was a limp barbed-wire fence, and then the woods began again. It was an open woods of beech and loblolly pine, and it was cut by deep cattle trails. We walked single file down a downhill trail. Some of the beeches were as big as New England village elms, but there was very little underbrush and very few understory trees, and almost no grass at all. That was the work of grazing cattle.

"I don't know," Borgman said. "This doesn't

look too bad. It's all been cut over and it's all been overgrazed, but I'm hopeful. The Monument could save it. It can still come back."

"It's better on down by the creek," Rosier said. "It's wilder down there in the bottom. But these woods are still alive. Hear that over yonder? Hear that paup-paup-paup? That's a pileated woodpecker sounding off. He isn't quite as shy as the ivorybill, but he's another bird that only likes deep woods."

"I think he's worth saving, too," Borgman said.

The cattle trail led down and down. The underbrush began to thicken, and the trees reached high overhead. We were in the creek bottom now. The air was hot and heavy, and there were puddles here and there in the mud of the trail. We skirted a grove of bony cypresses standing knee-deep in a black bayou. A little black skink twisted across the trail, and behind us a bullfrog croaked and gulped. Rosier stopped and looked around. We left the trail and broke through a stand of brush and briar and came out on the bank of Big Sandy Creek. It looked like a spring-fed creek. The water was brown and clear, and the sandy bottom was orange in the sunlight. I squatted down and put in my hand. I could feel the tug of the current, and the water was as cold as spring water.

"Big Sandy Creek," Borgman said. "You were right, Lance. This is real great. I like this rough topography. I certainly want to see some of this in the Monument."

"It's a right nice creek," Rosier said. "That hole down yonder is always full of channel cat. Big ones, too. They'll average two or three pounds."

"What about mushrooms?" Borgman said. "There ought to be mushrooms in here."

"Yes, sir," Rosier said. "There are — plenty of them. Every kind there is, almost. Or so they tell me. Mushrooms are something I never did learn. I tried one time. I sent away for a book. It cost me twenty-five dollars, and when it came I went out in the Thicket down near home, and I searched around, and pretty soon I found a nice-looking mushroom. It was a big old thing, and I remember it was all white. I dug it up as careful as I could and started home, and I hadn't got very far when I began to feel sick to my stomach. And then my head began to ache. I thought my head was going to bust open. But I finally got home and got out my book and looked up my mushroom, and I found it there, and I read what it said, and it said this was a mushroom that had a smell that would make a man sick. That was the end of me and mushrooms. I even gave up eating mushroom soup."

"I wonder what kind it was," Borgman said.

"I don't remember," Rosier said. "I gave the book away."

We walked on along the bank of the creek. I looked down into the catfish hole, but I couldn't see any fish. They were probably back under the bank. We followed the wandering course of the creek for about a hundred yards and then turned off. The undergrowth was too much. We cut across the bottom and found another cattle trail and started back up the hill. We came through a patch of mulberry brush and into a glade of flowers and soaring, pairing, mating butterflies. They were brown with bright-blue dots on the wingtips — mourning cloaks. The flowers were mostly the usual flowers of the Thicket, but there were some I didn't know. One was a little white flower with a fresh, old-fashioned look. I pointed it out to Rosier.

"That's a sundew," he said. "*Drosera rotundifolia*. It's a pretty little thing. Look at those little hairs on the leaves. Look how they shine. You'd swear they were drops of dew. They even fool the bugs. A bug comes alone and he sees that shining dew and he comes down to have himself a drink of water. But the hairs aren't dew, and they stick to him and he can't get away. He's caught. And then the sundew eats him."

It was one o'clock when we got back to the Williams Gro., and time we had some lunch. There was no place to eat but where we were, and we bought what we could — yellow cheese, Vienna sausages, bread, Dr Pepper — from a barefooted woman in the store, and took it outside and ate at a table in the shade of a live-oak tree. It was good to sit down, and somewhere up in a tree a mockingbird whistled like a cardinal and called like a wren. The ground under

the table was paved with a thousand bottle caps —
soda-pop caps. This was a bone-dry county.

We finished lunch, and Borgman lighted a thick
cigar. "I guess we ought to get going," he said. "I'd
like to take a look at Tight-Eye before we call it a
day."

"I'd like to show it to you," Rosier said. "I'll
take you in and show you the Witness Tree. Maybe
you've heard of it. The Witness Tree is a big magnolia tree that marks the corner where Liberty County
and Hardin County and Polk County all meet. The
experts say it's a thousand years old. I want you to
see it."

"Why do they call it Tight-Eye?" I said.

"I reckon because it's so thick," he said. "You
can't walk through it with your eyes wide open. The
branches and brambles would put them out. It's the
thickest part of the Thicket."

We dropped the remains of our lunch in a box in
front of the store and got in the car and circled back
to the crossroads and headed down another gravel
highway. There was a big *No Dumping* sign on the
right, and piles of trash and garbage, and the trees
for a hundred yards around were plastered with
windblown papers. We passed the endless gash of
a pipeline right-of-way. We passed two miles of forest
marked with the sky-blue blaze of a lumber company, and then a mile blazed in orange. We passed a
billboard: MODEL HOMES. We passed a sudden
pasture and a fallen-down log cabin. Then we turned

off the highway and onto a narrow, potholed asphalt
road. The trees came together high overhead, and
the asphalt road gave way to sandy mud. We were
well into Tight-Eye now. We drove for another ten
or fifteen minutes. The only car we met was a station
wagon with Louisiana plates.

Rosier sat up and cleared his throat. "I reckon
this will do," he said. "We'll get out here and walk in
to the famous Witness Tree."

A track that had once been a logging road led
into the Tight-Eye woods. The track was overgrown
with red oak and sweet-gum saplings, and hedged
with broomstick pine. It wasn't much more than a
crack in the forest wall.

"This is real Thicket," Borgman said. "This is
the best I've seen today. This is what we want for the
Monument."

"Yes, sir," Rosier said. "And we'll be right in the
middle of it in just about a minute. This track
doesn't go where we're going." He had his eyes on
the trees ahead on the right. He hesitated, moved on
again, and stopped. "This is it," he said. "There's
the old survey blaze. We go across country now."

We broke off the track and into the flanking
woods. It *was* real Thicket — a forest floor of fallen
trees swamped with brush and briar, an understory
of holly and dogwood and gum and oak and maple
and hawthorn trailing vines and Spanish moss, and a
soaring, pillared canopy of beech and magnolia and
loblolly pine. There was no sky, no sun, no sense of

direction. We climbed over logs and circled sloughs and ducked under hanging branches, and every log and every slough and every branch looked very much like the last. There were no landmarks. There were only the double welts of the old blazes. We picked our way from blaze to blaze — missing a blaze and circling back and finding it and moving on to the next. We walked for a mile and a half. Then a kind of clearing appeared. It was a grassy clearing with a big gray stump full of woodpecker holes and a tumble of big vine-covered logs. Rosier stopped and kicked around in the grass at the edge of the clearing and uncovered a wooden stake — an ironclad boundary stake.

"Here we are," he said. "This is the county corner. Ernest is standing in Hardin County, and you're in Polk County, and I'm over here in Liberty County." He turned and pointed at the stump. "And that's the famous and historic Witness Tree."

"That *stump?*" I said. It was a very big stump. It was fifty feet high and at least four feet in diameter. But still it was just a stump. "That stump is the Witness Tree?"

Borgman was staring at it, too. "What happened, Lance?" he said.

"They poisoned it three years ago," Rosier said. "They pumped it full of lead arsenate. I can show you the holes they bored to put in the poison. I came in with the experts that made the investigation. We found the holes stopped up with little wooden pegs."

"But why?" I said. "Why would anybody do a thing like that?"

"It sounds crazy," Borgman said.

"Yes, sir," Rosier said. "But there isn't any mystery about it. They did it for a warning. They were some of the folks that don't want the Monument."

ROUECHE, BERTON
AUTHOR
WHAT'S LEFT
TITLE

361
AN

DATE DUE	
	BORROWER'S NAME